# ABANDONED NORTH CASCADES

# ABANDONED NORTH CASCADES

## NATURE TAKES BACK IN WASHINGTON

DEBRA HURON

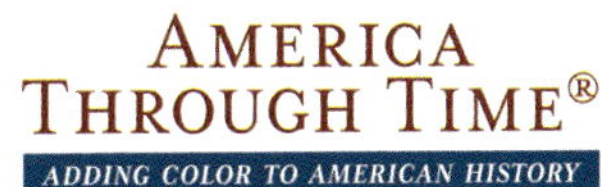

America Through Time is an imprint of Fonthill Media LLC
www.through-time.com
office@through-time.com

Published by Arcadia Publishing by arrangement with Fonthill Media LLC
For all general information, please contact Arcadia Publishing:
Telephone: 843-853-2070
Fax: 843-853-0044
E-mail: sales@arcadiapublishing.com
For customer service and orders:
Toll-Free 1-888-313-2665

www.arcadiapublishing.com

First published 2021



ISBN 978-1-63499-350-0



Typeset in Trade Gothic 10pt on 15pt
Printed and bound in England

# CONTENTS

# ACKNOWLEDGMENTS

First and foremost, I would like to thank my family for their support. My father for not killing me for all the adventures I have taken. My sister and brother-in-law, Theresa and Vjeko, for always having my back and helping reassure my decisions to my father every time.

Each destination had its perfect crew that I owe tribute too:

Iggy, for bringing me to my first abandoned building, even though I was honestly terrified.

Kristin, my best friend, who was always down to urban explore with me; we have so much more in store to see.

Frosh, Zucca, Georgi, Roman, and Steve, my spooky Gatorade crew; these moments will play on repeat in my head forever.

Stein and Shannee', my King's Park models; you made my photography seem easy.

Jurski, for helping me successfully finish my first abandoned photography project.

Tom, to whom I owe so much, you are the best critique (and somewhat too much of a critique), but you offer me a different visual eye that I am forever grateful for.

And last but not least, Alie, Ali, and Robyn, for joining me on this specific journey; thanks for being the best last-minute squad I never knew I needed.

I would not have it any other way and I hope the adventures never end.

# INTRODUCTION

Look deep into nature, and then you will understand everything better;" wise words from Albert Einstein. It is truly hard to deny the positive effect and reaction of nature on the human brain. Multiple studies have shown that exposure to nature can not only trigger emotionally positive reactions, it can improve physical health, reducing one's stress hormones, heart rate, blood pressure, and even muscle tension. As far back as the Middle Ages, monasteries for those with mental illnesses offered restorative gardens for their patients to facilitate nature's benefits of healing. Psychiatric wards can date as far back as AD 872, where a hospital in Cairo provided music therapy for the mentally ill. However, it was not until the 1800s that architects would use the principles behind restorative gardens on choosing new sites for mental hospitals. They would design wards to have beautiful courtyards, with an array of many delectable colors, and serene surroundings to support the natural healing elements of nature. Patients would be encouraged to take a stroll, to take in the world's many delights that in other types of businesses may have been overlooked. By 1838, the Hanwell Insane Asylum began a rehabilitation treatment that would allow the patient to do chores or work and, in short, be rewarded for bittersweet indulgences, like beer. It was an easy quick of the trade; in exchange, patients in the process were able to receive fresh air, daylight, and be able to exercise from their daily tasks.

During this time, gold nuggets were discovered in Sacramento valley in 1848, sparking the beginning of the Gold Rush. Little did we know that the events that followed would shape the western front of Industrial American history as we know it. The news spread fast and the Gold Rush became the largest mass migration in United States history, even attracting immigrants from around the world. Early settlers and miners helped flourish these communities from the ground up, building structures and starting families of their own. Multiple railroad lines were also being constructed that made it easier to travel or trade from anywhere in these states. Industries like lumber, agriculture, mining, fur, manufacturing, and transportation grew overnight. By 1888, the Northern Pacific railroad line reached the Puget Sound linking the distance between the East Coast to the Pacific Northwest territories. The following year, Washington was granted statehood, after a thirteen-year hiatus of any state joining the union.

At this point, the Gold Rush craze was approaching its end of days until the Klondike Gold Rush in Alaska caused a final uproar that fueled the economy in these Pacific Northwest towns. Though it took a year for anyone to even know of its existence because of the distance and lack of communication in these times, when word finally reached Seattle, the news traveled fast. Seattle businesses seized the opportunity to franchise by praising the stories of the rich and exploited the newcomers traveling from far by boat across the Atlantic. It did not take long for Seattle to franchise on the opportunity. Those with port status would boost and praise the stories of the rich, exploiting newcomers traveling by boat across the Atlantic. "Gateway to the Gold Fields," port merchants would chant loudly for those hungry for gold and all that would follow. The Puget Sound's role in trade would grow so much that it caused an effect on the speed of population growth as well. In 1890, Puget Sound had 75,000 residents, by 1910, the amount of people there grew fourteen times that original number to 1.1 million people.

The Gold Rush played a huge role in the Pacific Northwest's development. The economy was booming. Business was good.

As the 1900s approached, those on the quest for gold reached a plateau. These areas either no longer bore gold left worth finding or never had it all. These miners utilized all their resources and there was no purpose to remain in their locations, which they alone were in the majority of creating. The true winners of the Gold Rush were those who were able to afford the expenses of sifting equipment, meaning the rich just got richer. Many cities founded by miners were left abandoned. Those who chose to stay utilized their own skills and adapted to their environment to start a new life of their own. These factors set the tone for the cities and structures of the Pacific Northwest, and these towns were built overnight by high demand in this timeframe. Washington was booming, the forests were dense and abundant, and the social structures of society were growing. The North Cascades, also known as the American Alps, were on the verge of its long-awaited journey, of a story worth being told on how it got to where it is today.

Mother Nature is not a force to be reckoned with; she has always had her ways in this world. Though many have tried, not every community can overcome the sense of defeat that comes from nature. Weather can change patterns, cities will flood, industries will become obsolete, and people will migrate. The true purpose is to find enlightenment in our pasts and respect what once was. We may not understand it, but we are here today because of it. Abandoned structures offer us the not-so-glamorous history book we never knew we needed.

I hope this book presents you with the reality or the truth of what life has offered before you. I hope it reveals a type of madness of what our reality is when we are gone. That life has its own plans for things and we may think we have a plan, but in reality, you can either live gently or ride the waves thrown at us. So the real question is, do you want to ride?

# 1

# NORTHERN HOSPITAL FOR THE INSANE

The definition of what mental health is will change throughout our lifespan. At the beginning of the nineteenth century, a mental institution's purpose was meant to confine those deemed mentally ill from the public's eye. Some of the conditions that would make one be considered mentally ill would be head injuries, epilepsy, alcoholism, homosexuality, outspoken women, post-menopause wives, or children who likely had ADHD.

By 1909, the National Committee for Mental Hygiene was founded by leading American psychiatrist Adolf Meyer, with efforts from a former mental patient Clifford W. Beers. Today recognized as Mental Health America, it ensures to improve living conditions, attitudes, and services for those living with mental health conditions. Since then, mental hygiene has been redefined and recognized more than ever today—it has had a lot of time

During the same timeline, Washington only had two mental hospitals—Eastern State and Western State—which both reached capacity. To comply with the overcrowding concerns, the plans for Northern Hospital for the Insane became established in 1909. The Olmsted Brothers landscaping architecture firm signed on to master the plan of the 1,100-acre property into a state-of-the-art self-sustaining rehabilitation campus for the clinically insane. The Olmsted Brothers, who were founding members of the American Society of Landscape Architects, played prominent roles in the development of the National Park Service; they were sons to the renowned architect Frederick Law Olmsted, designer of New York's Central Park.

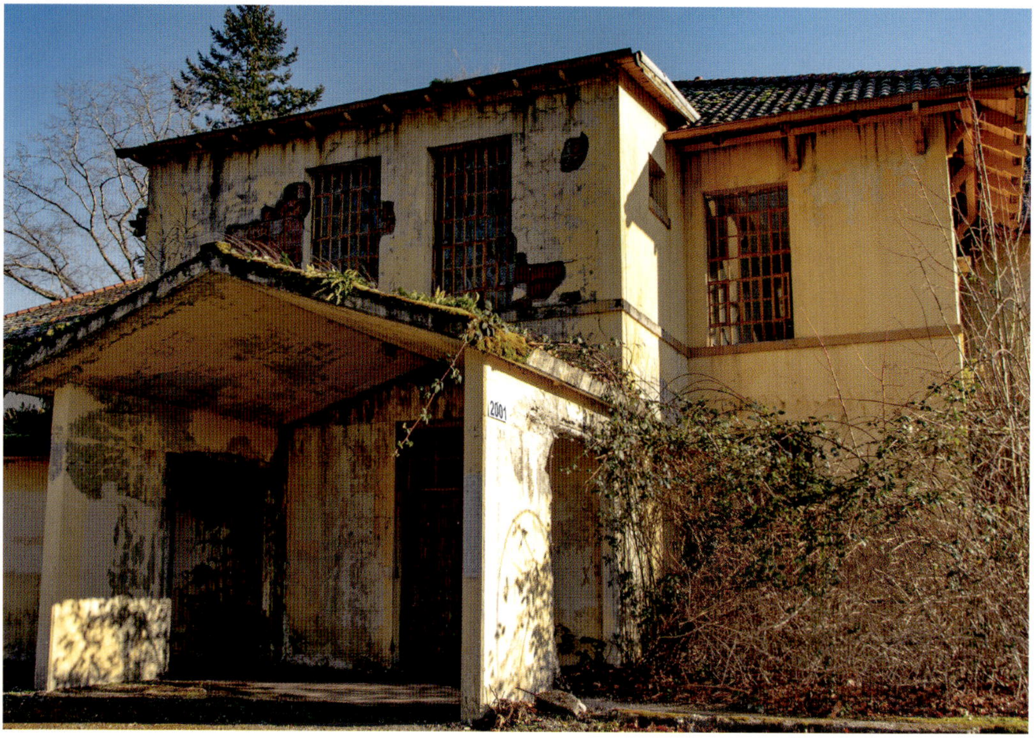

An entrance to the former ward on the Northern State property.

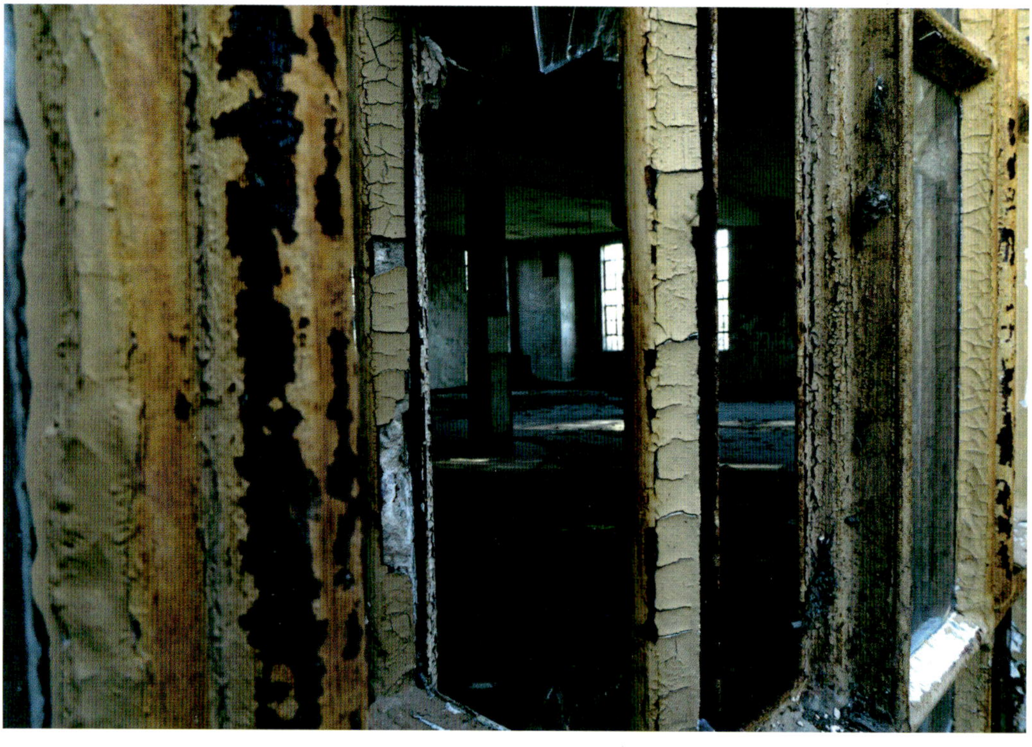

The paint peels and rusts on old broken glass windows.

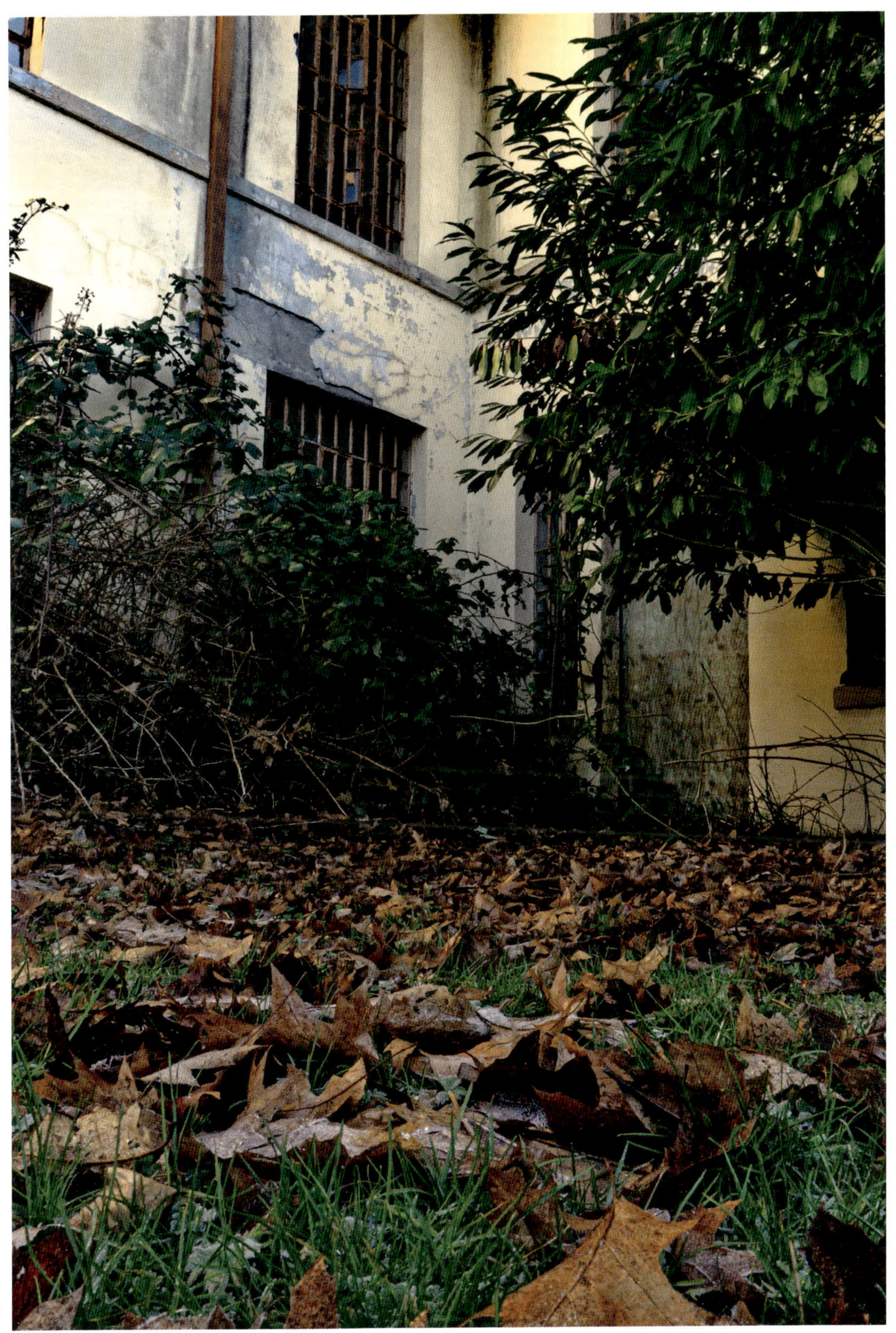

Boarded-up doors and overgrown weeds block old possibly entryways.

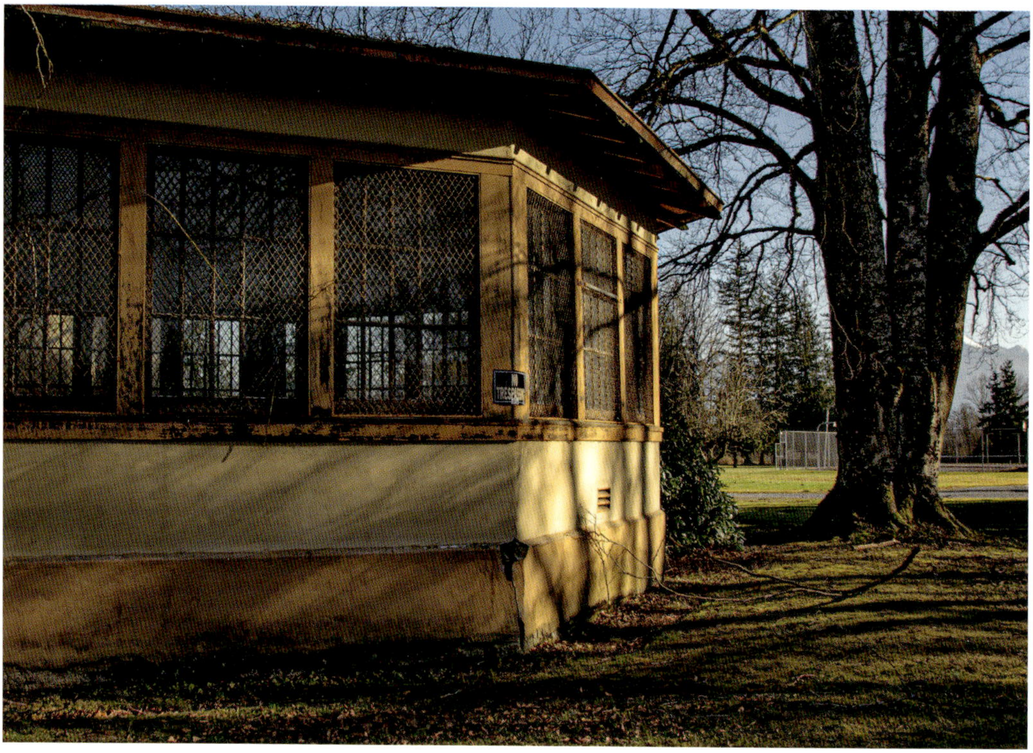

Building extension to the Northern Hospital that gave patients the ability to look outward the scenery.

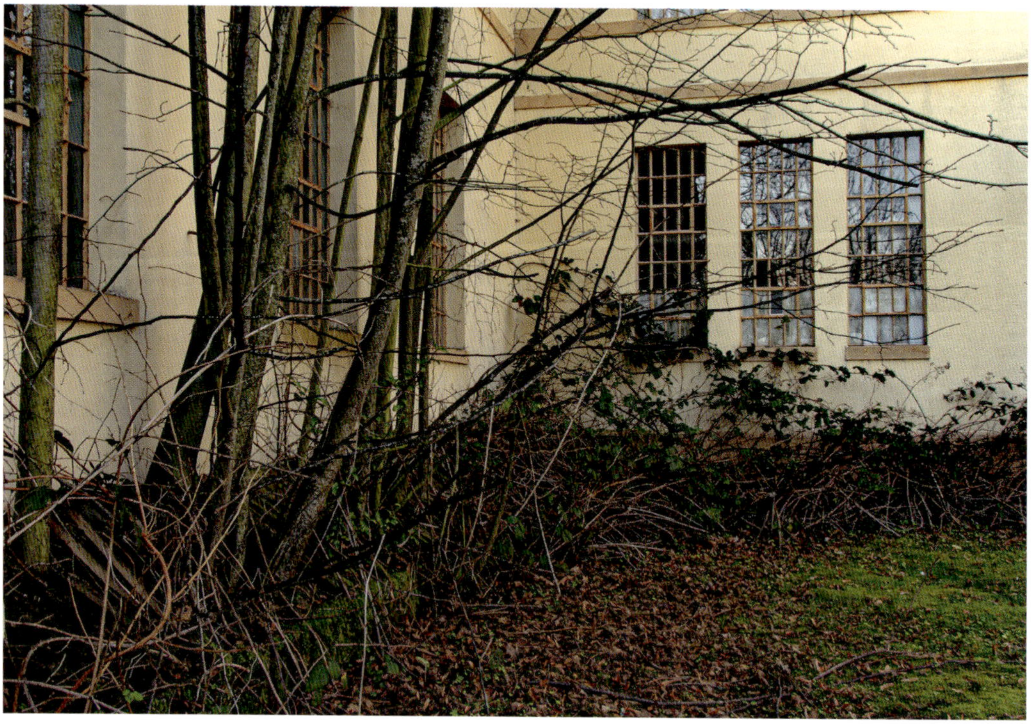

Boarded-up basement windows with trees growing between the boards.

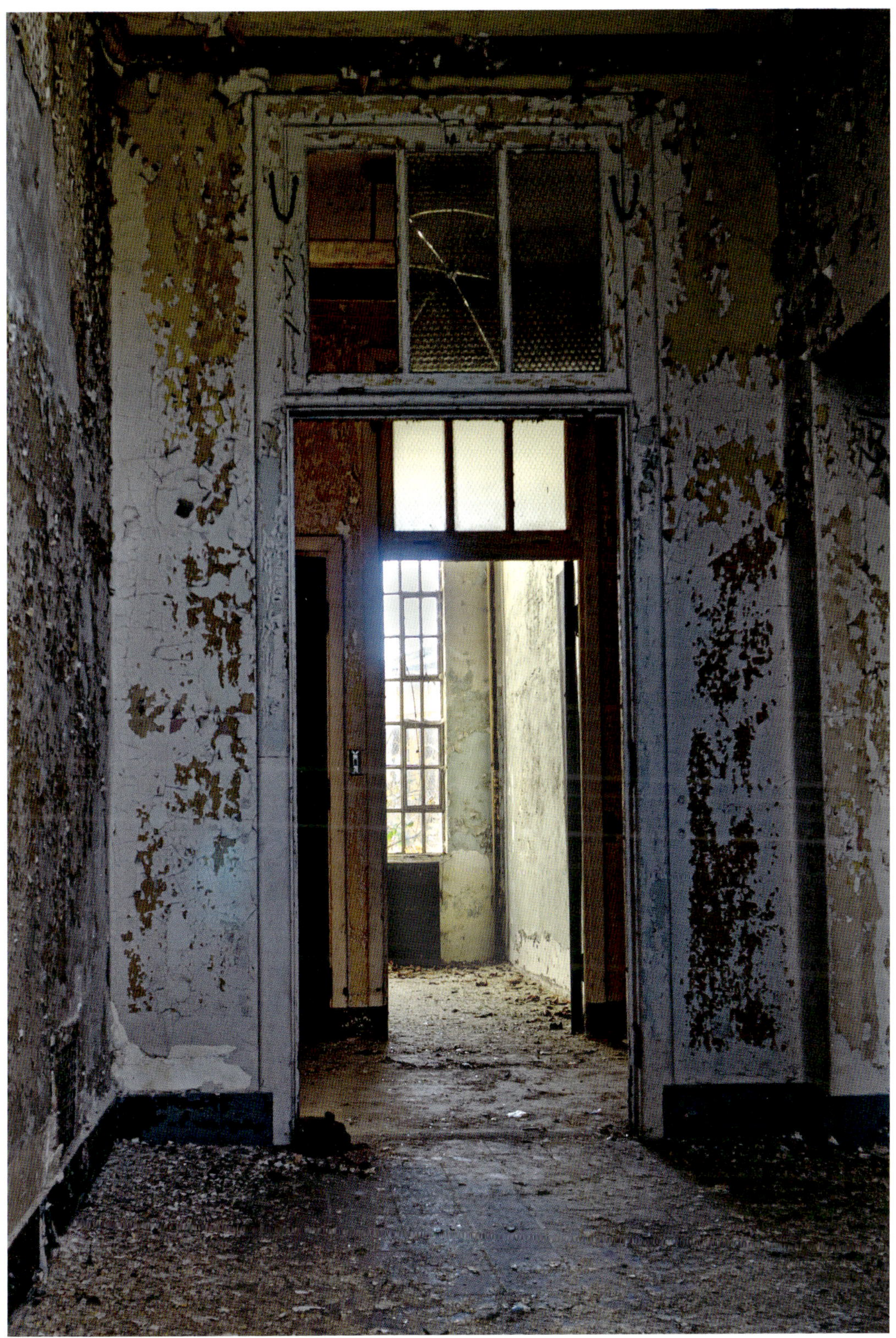

Peeling paint chips with doorways missing and glass shattered across the floor.

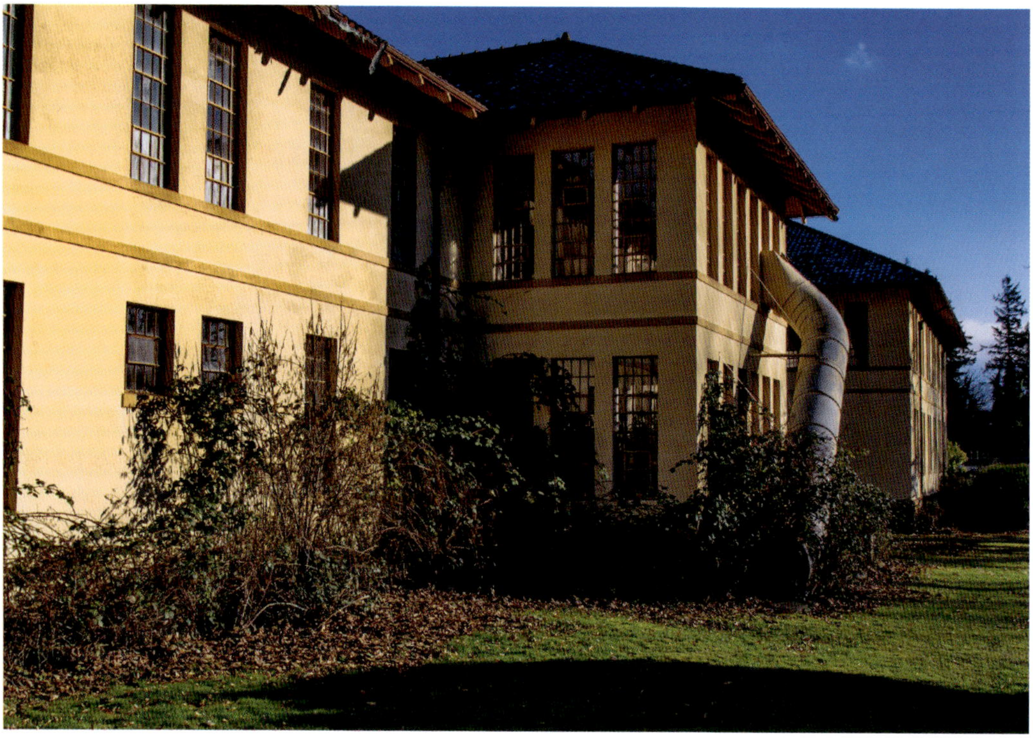

Somewhere along the outside corridor of the campus.

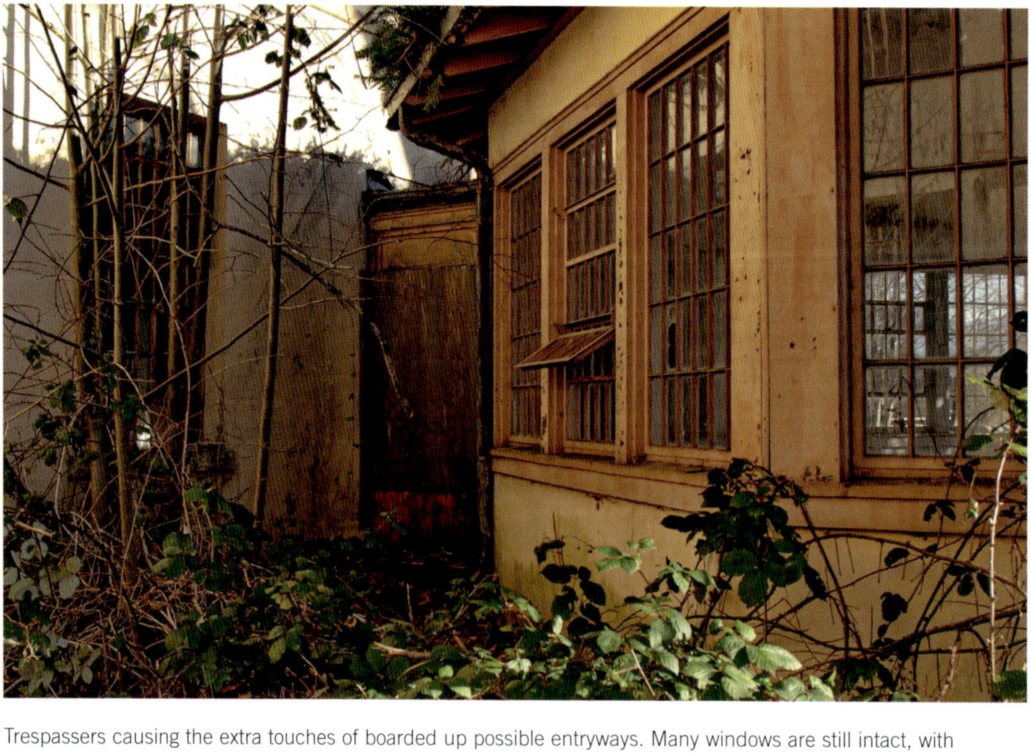

Trespassers causing the extra touches of boarded up possible entryways. Many windows are still intact, with thorns distracting any of those interested in getting inside.

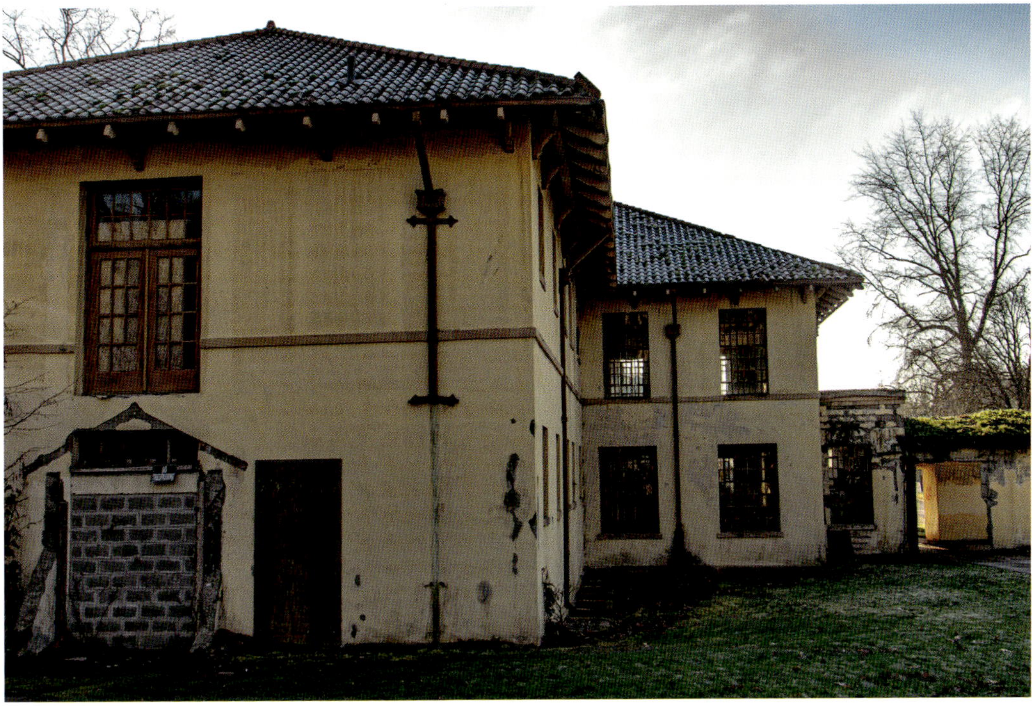

Layers of concrete, wood, and brick patch along the campus walls with different streams of colors. The property offers a unique display of history decaying.

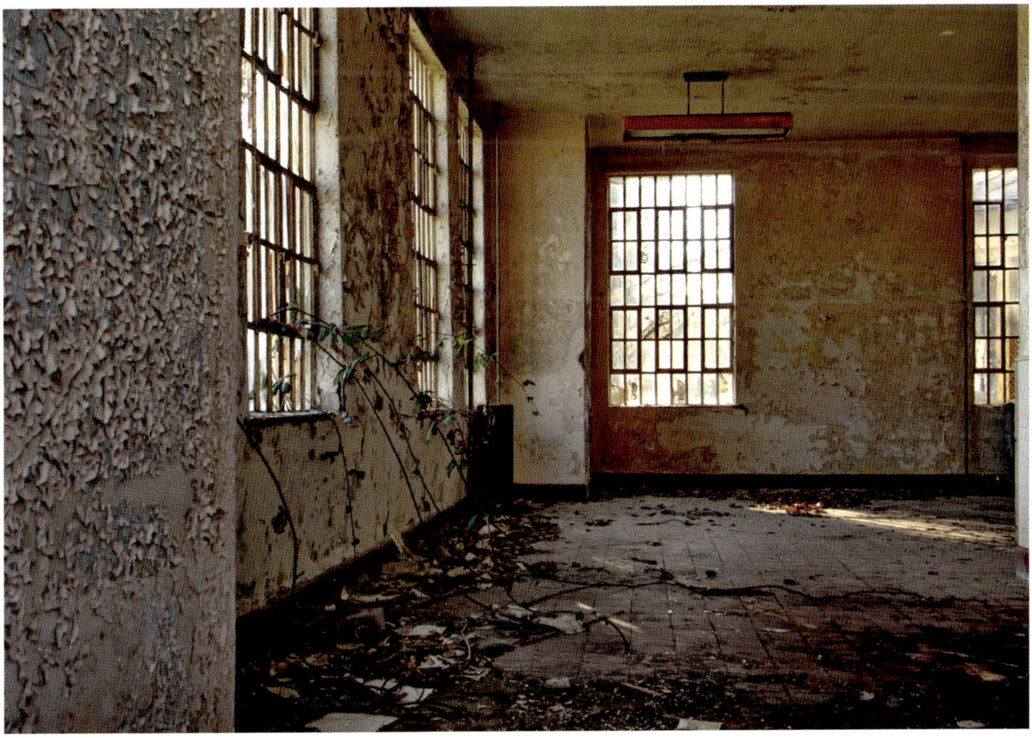

So many patients have lived in these dimly lit rooms now taken over as vines flow downward through windows.

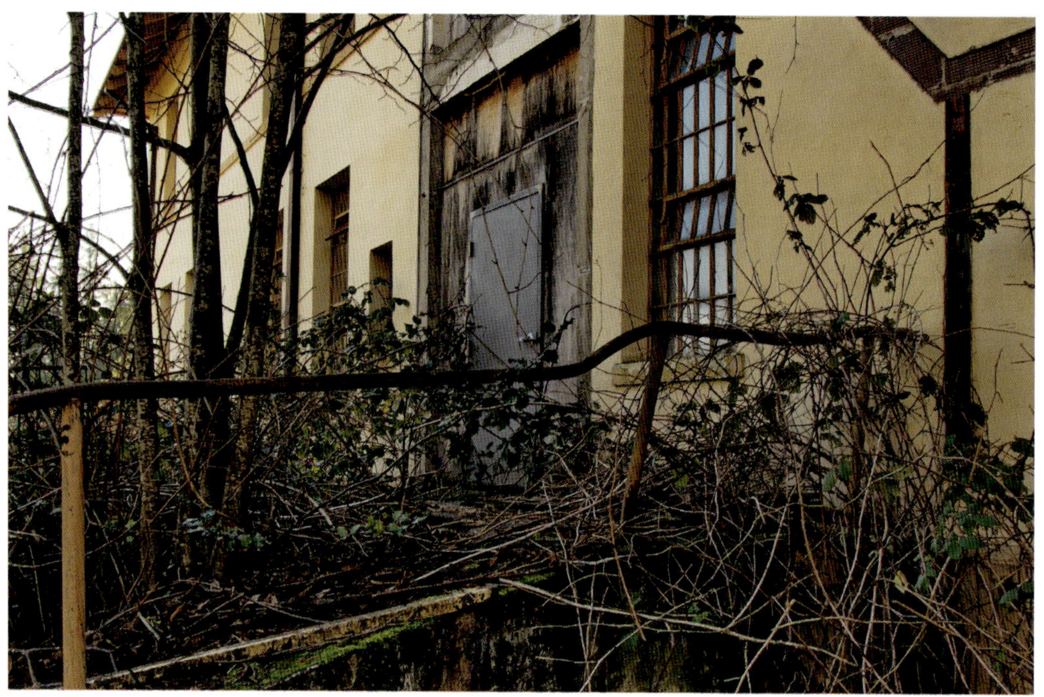

The mental health practices of the past were abandoned the same ways the buildings were, practically overnight. Lobotomies will never be treated the same.

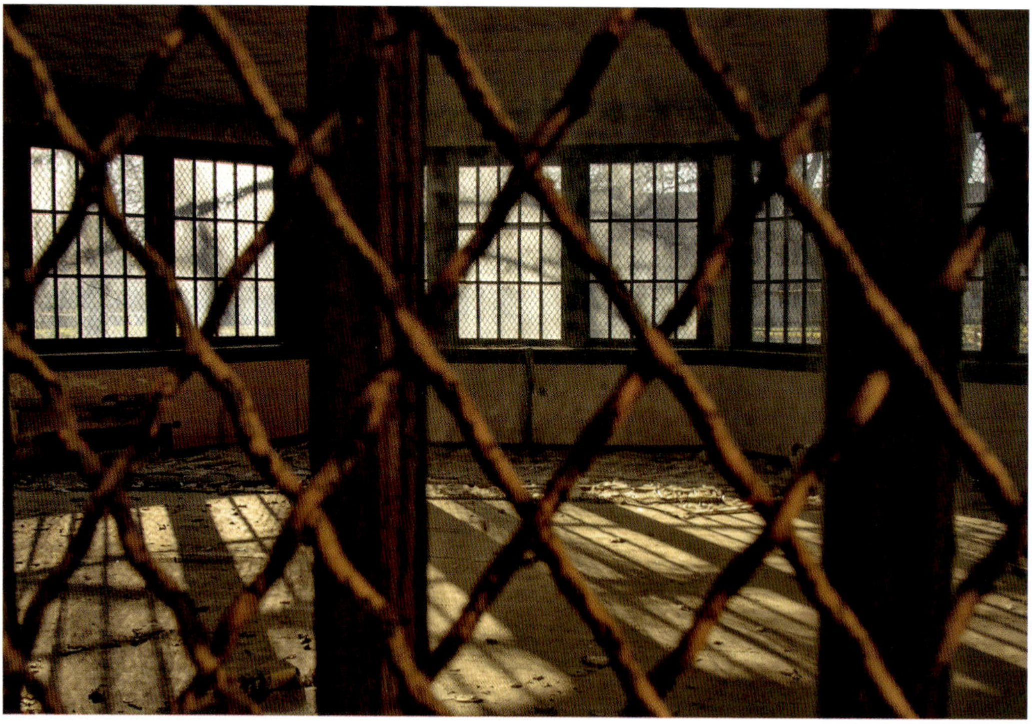

Hexagon rooms with only one entryway into the main buildings, let the patients look outwards into the landscapes and gardens.

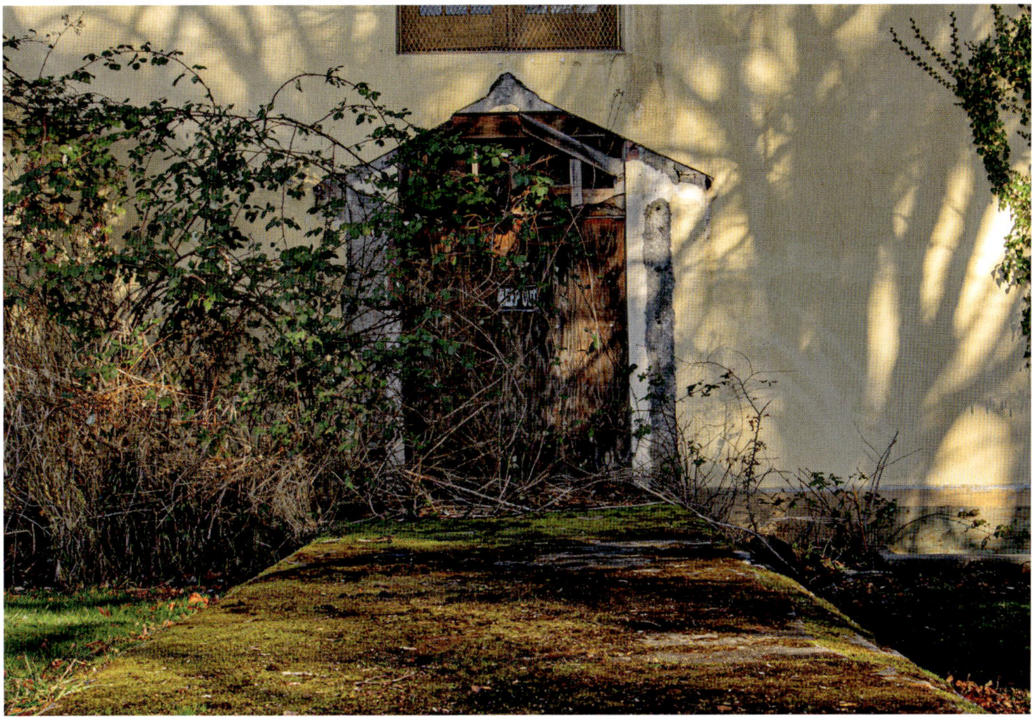

Leaves and branches block double doorways with an almost kingdom-like feel.

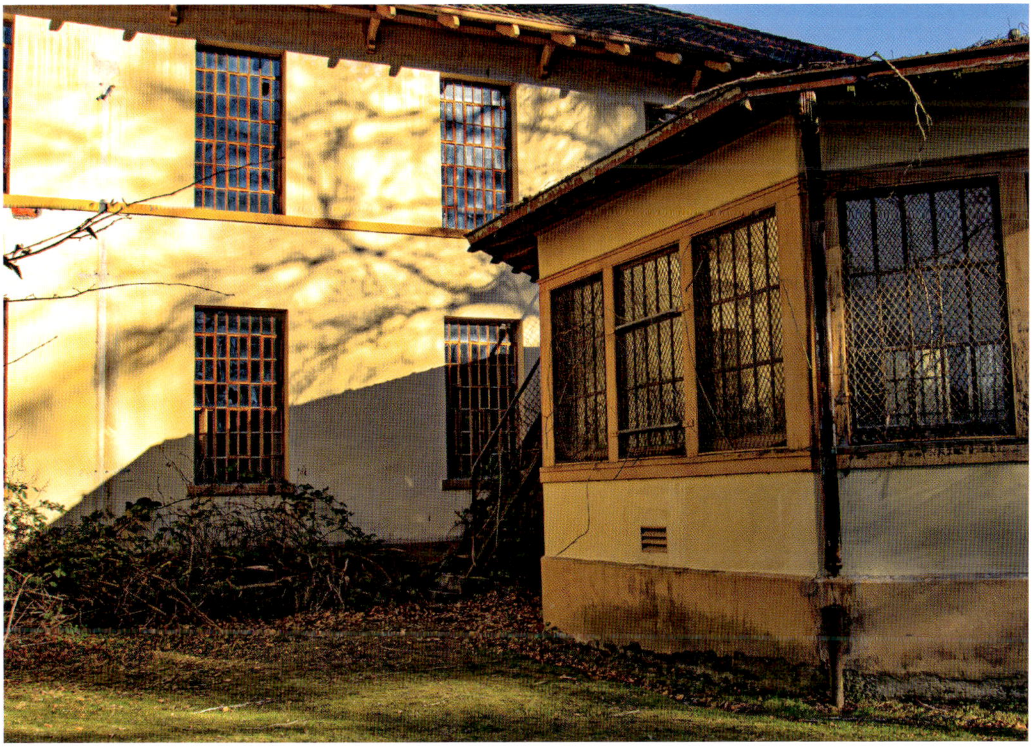

Hexagon rooms exterior, offering a full surrounding view of the property.

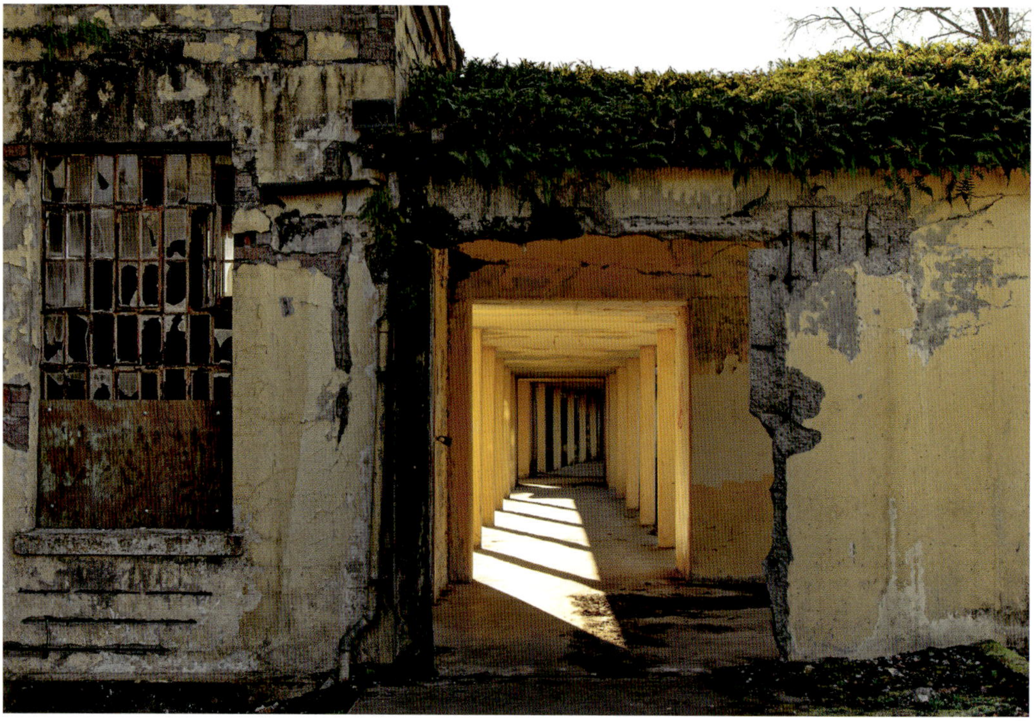

The architecture of the buildings were constructed with Spanish Colonial influence and have beautiful symmetrical corridors for those traveling between buildings.

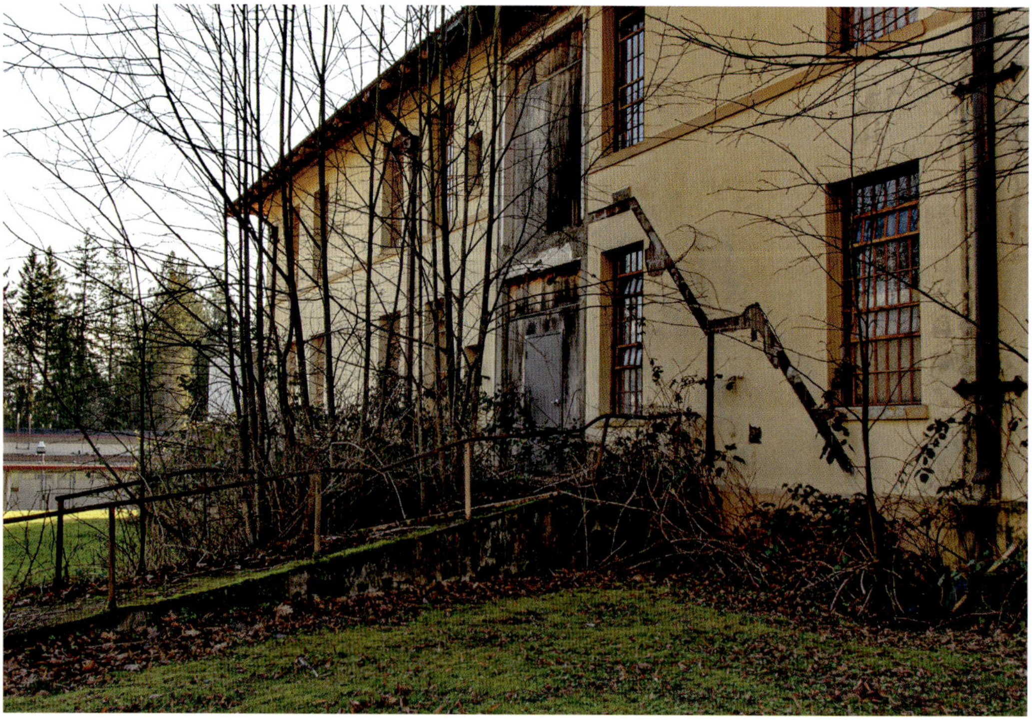

A handicap-accessible entryway with moss now consuming the ground.

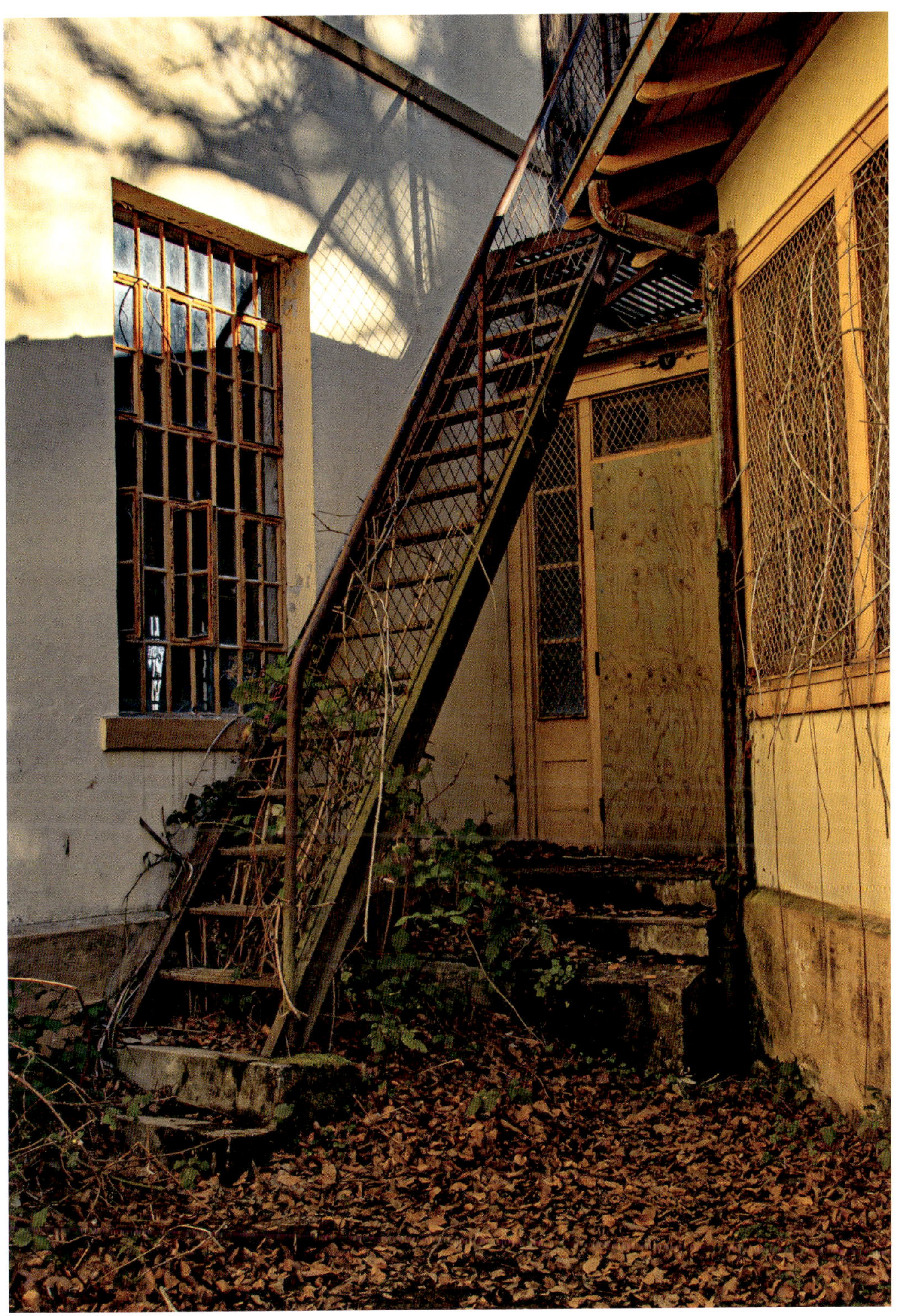

Metal staircase along the courtyards to an easy second floor accessible, now not seeming so ideal for an entryway for modern mental hospitals.

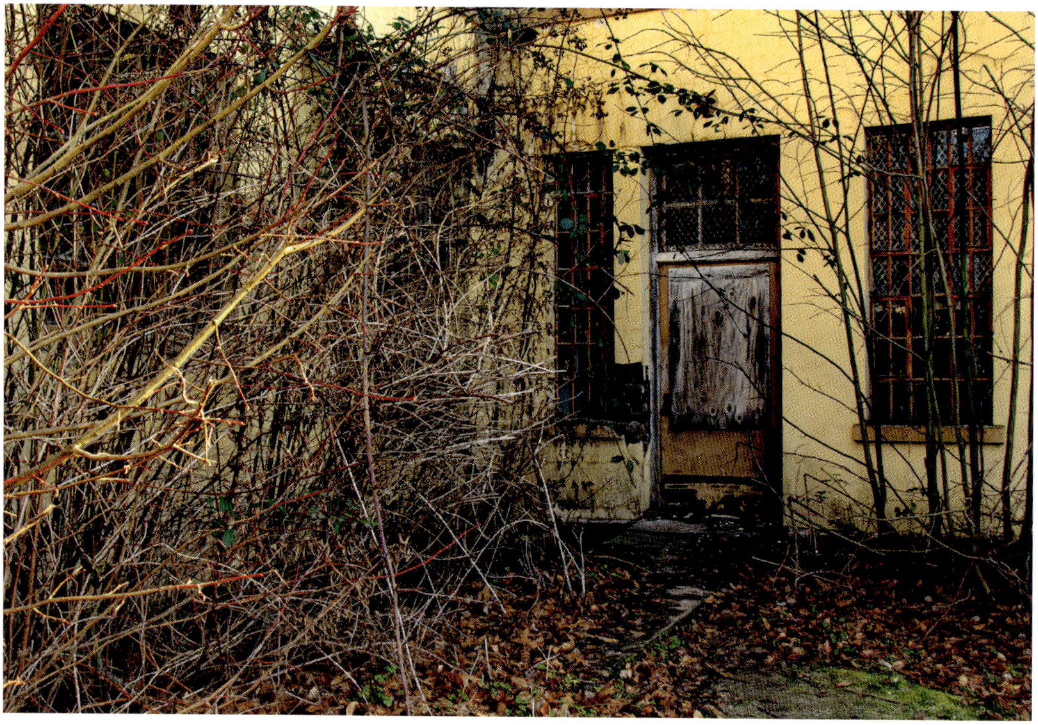

Private back entryway to the main hospital for special facilities.

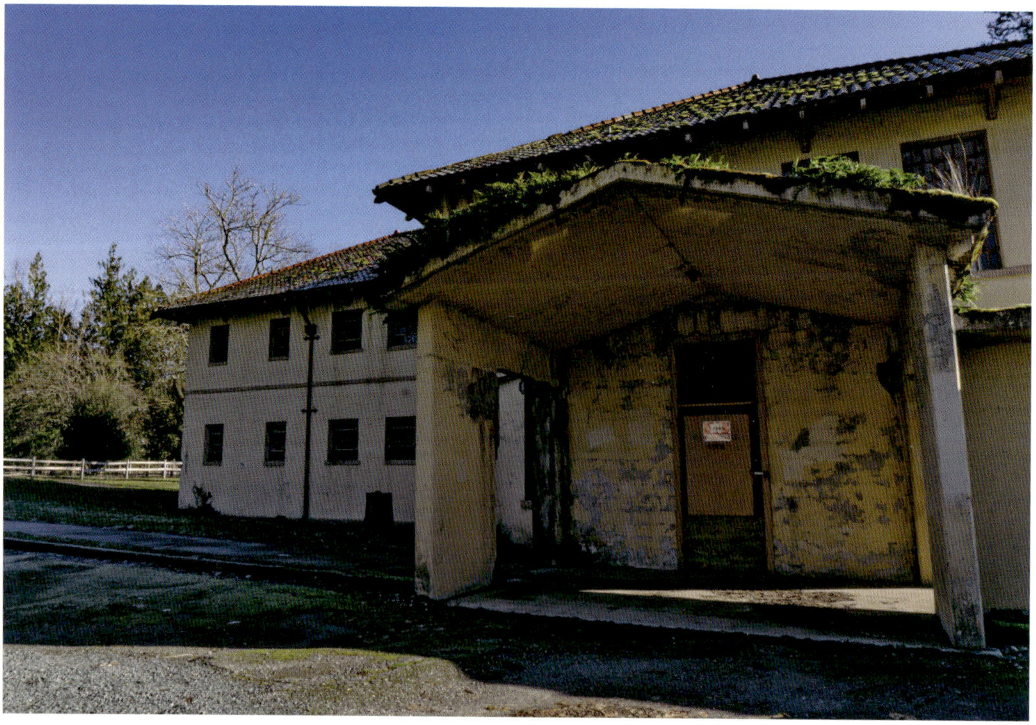

Some of the buildings display a slow coming of nature winning, or some with nature defeating with structures barely standing.

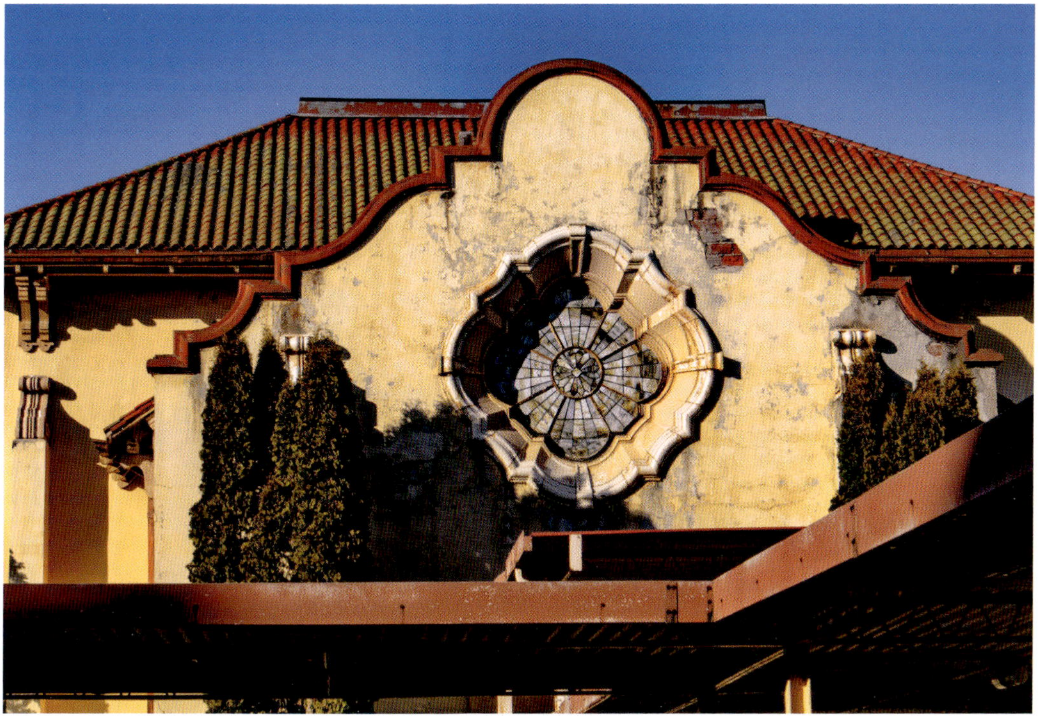

*Above:* This building's purpose was an assembly hall that would host dances for the patients trying to live what they thought to be a "normal life."

*Right:* Even the material holding the window panes has now fully deteriorated, causing wood to block intruders.

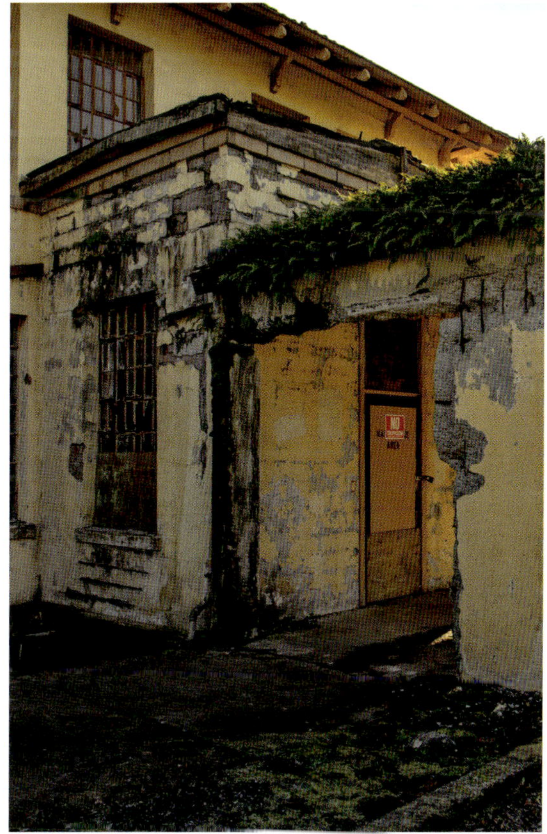

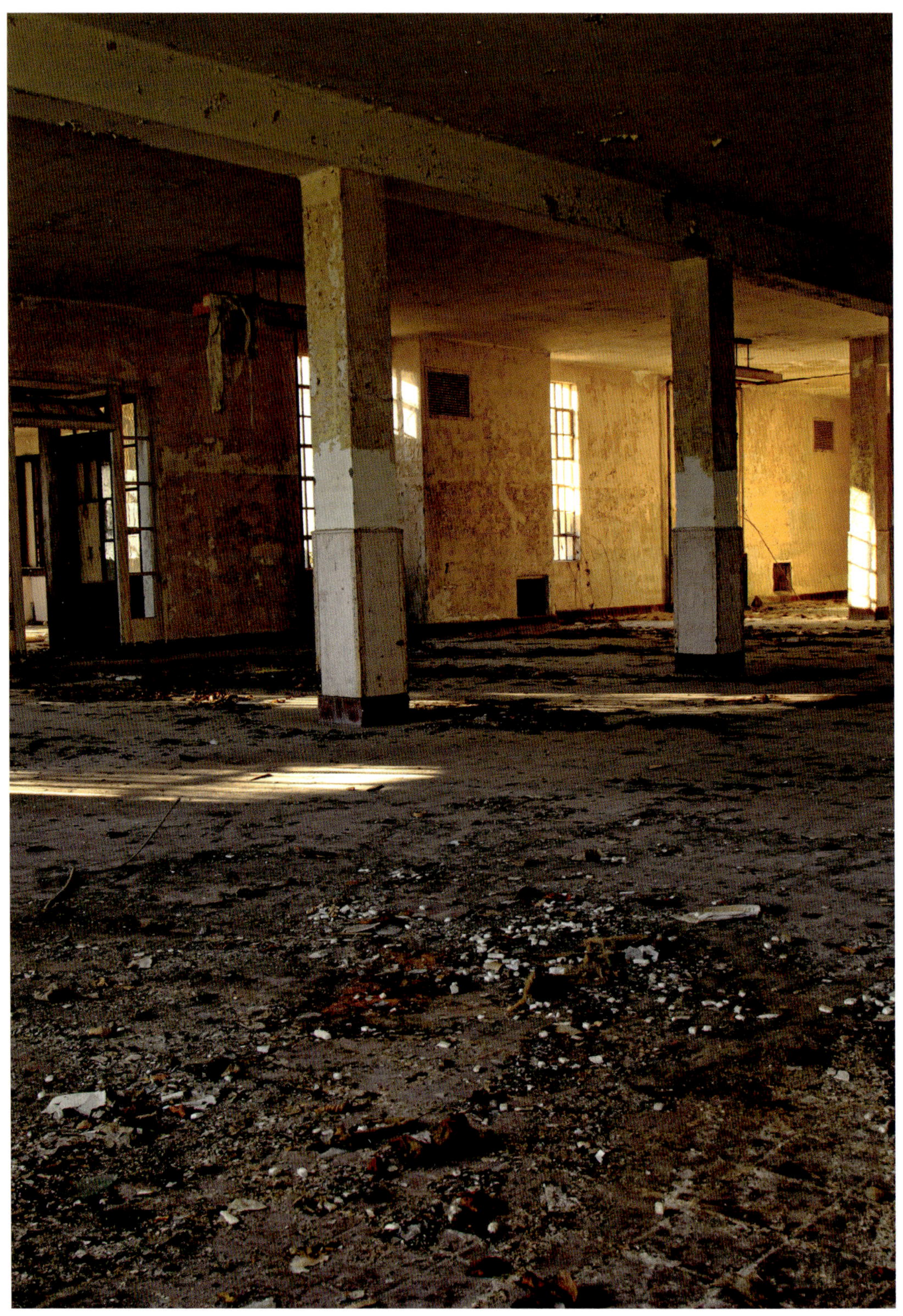

Wide open rooms bare paint chips and missing paint lacquer on the walls in certain areas, displaying how fast they were to take every little thing out of these buildings with no second thought to ever come back or paint over.

The property was orchestrated with stucco-style buildings and courtyards influenced by Spanish colonial architecture, ideally situated in hot climates. The campus included sites to collaborate with the ideology of it being self-sustaining like its 700-acre dairy farm for raising livestock and growing vegetables in which the patients would work on. The other 500 acres included staff and patient housing, bakery, dining hall, canning facility, greenhouse, sewage system, water reservoir, steam plant, quarry, lumber mill, laundry, library, gymnasium, crematorium, and cemetery. The campus itself was a closed collaborated little city unto itself that had no purpose for the outside world.

On May 25, 1912, the hospital opened its doors, throwing a celebration for families dropping off loved ones, welcoming the patients to their new home. Northern Hospital for the Insane became the largest asylum in Washington State, with people being sent from eight different counties. Patients were treated with occupational therapy in hopes that it would normalize their routines and reform their behaviors.

Patients were encouraged to attend dances, play games like shuffleboard, shop in the town, and work on the property. Northern Hospital was built in a town formerly known as Bug, so for the sixty-seven years of it being open, the locals referred to it as the "bug house." Northern Hospital was a training hospital for medical staff with the newest medical trials of drugs, treatments, therapies, and surgeries. Though Northern Hospital established an exquisite reputation for its medical developments of their time, in current times, these things would seem barbaric. Treatments would include electric-shock therapy, insulin-coma therapies, experimental drugs (some of which cause heavy sedation), and, by the 1940s, trans-orbital lobotomies. It is unfortunate to admit that not all of these inmates, referred to as patients, should have been there. Some men reportedly committed their wives or children just for disagreements for their outspoken behavior. In its peak, Northern Hospital housed over 415 staff members and 2,200 patients in the 1950s.

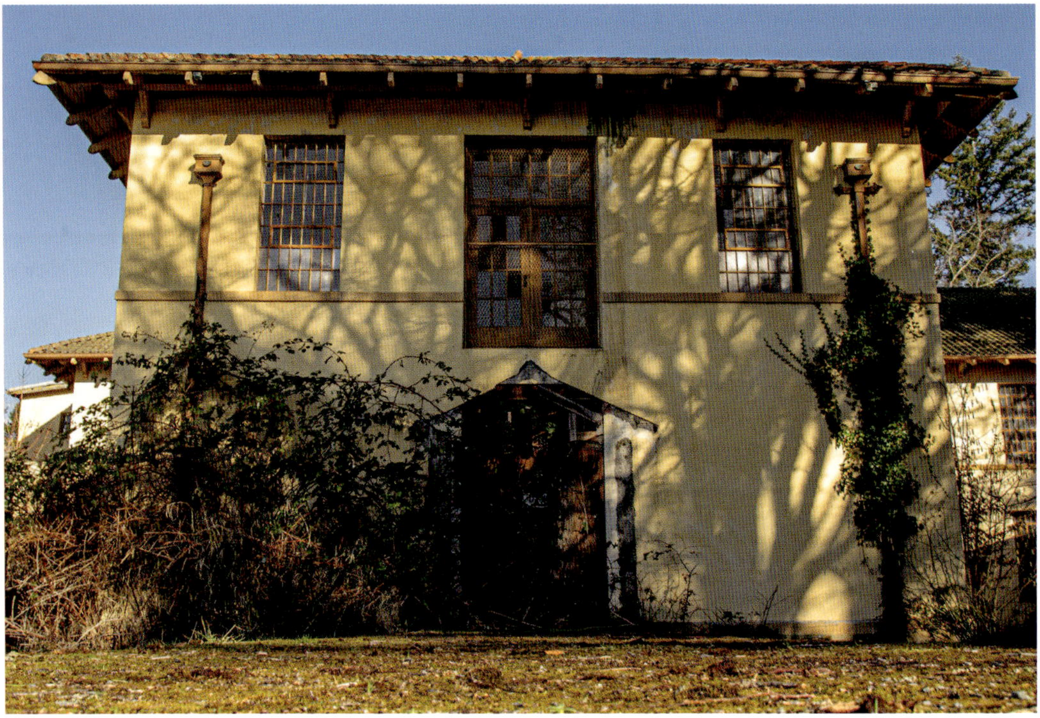

Although having been abandoned for over fifty years now, the buildings still look as great as can be for their age.

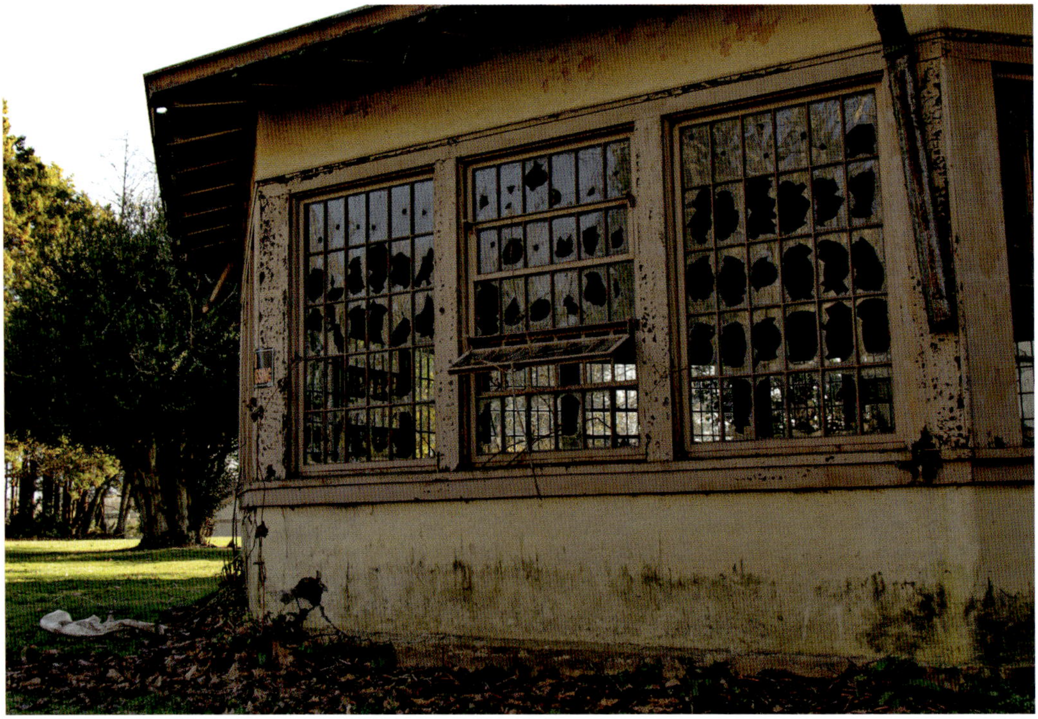

Unfortunately with beautiful abandoned structures, vandalism goes hand in hand, as mischievous trespassers destroy old windows with rocks.

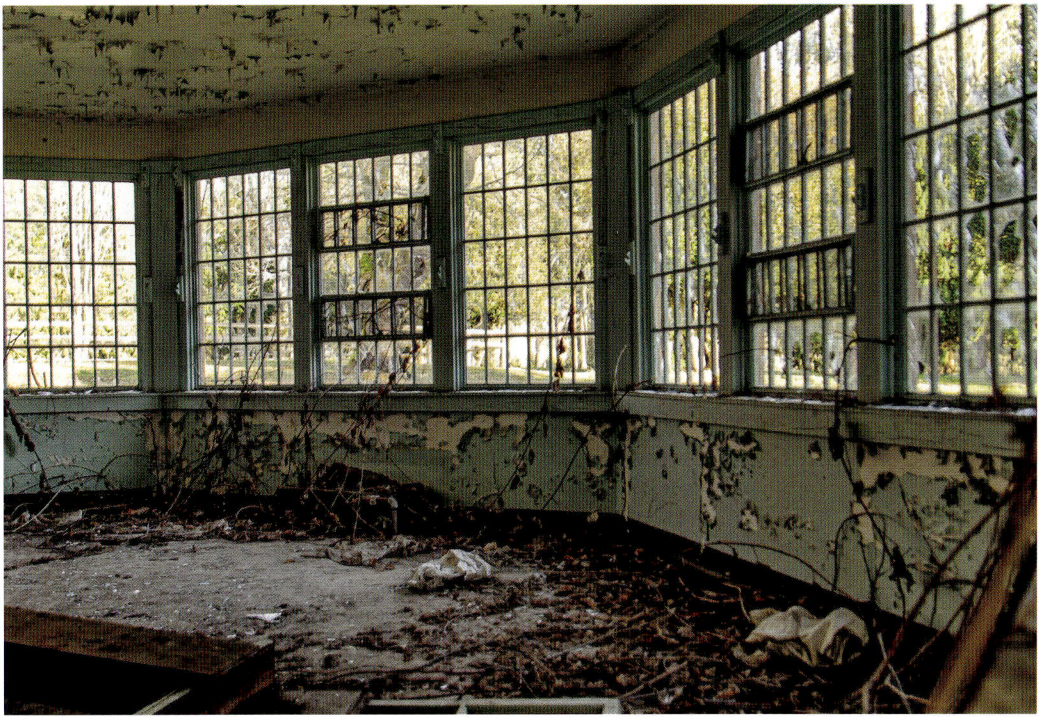

Once foam green walls now peel over, and branches and broken glass lines the floor.

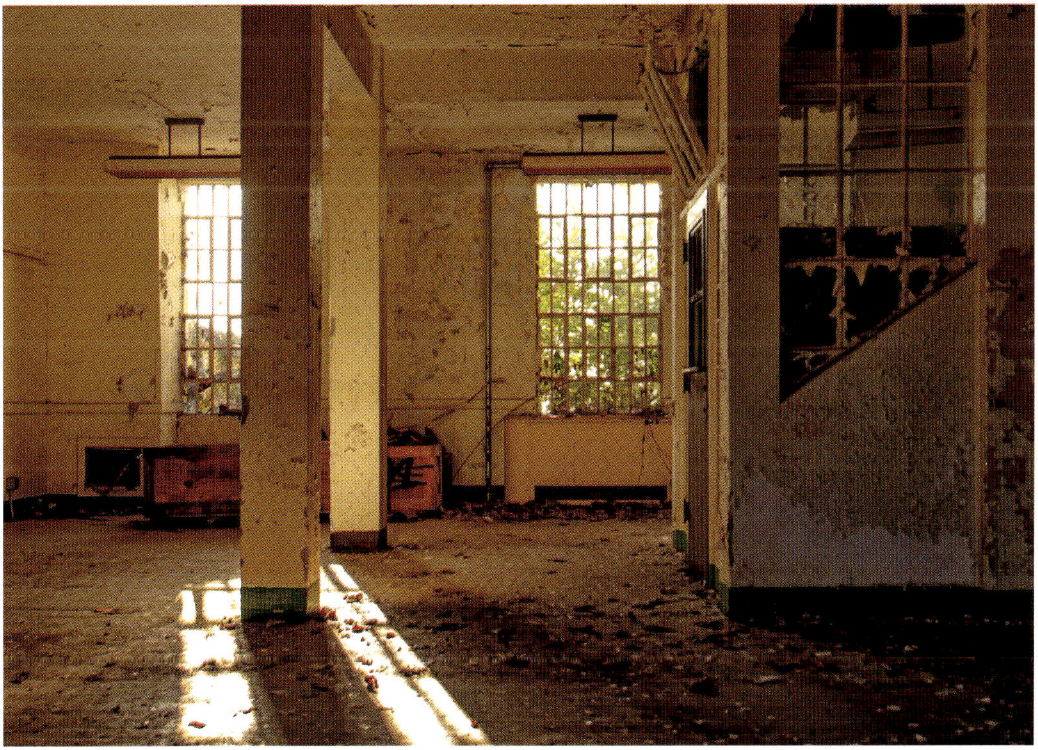

Main entryways to facilities common rooms where different types of treatment would occur.

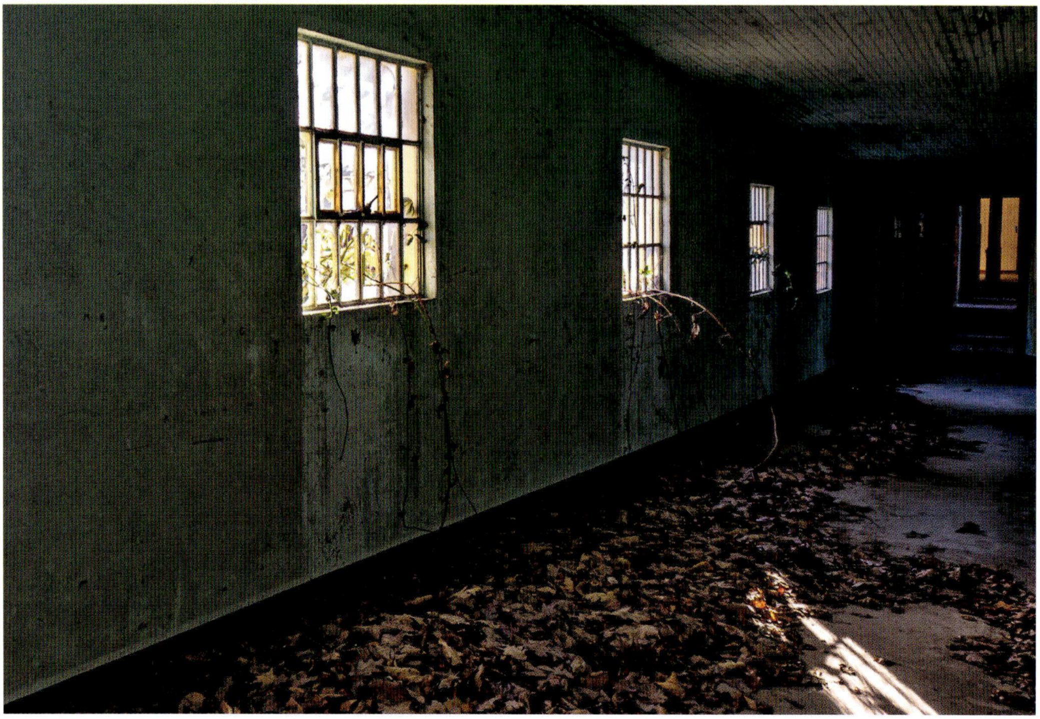

Locals tell ghost stories, most popularly of a little girl wandering around the campus looking for her red ball and then another of a man looking for said girl.

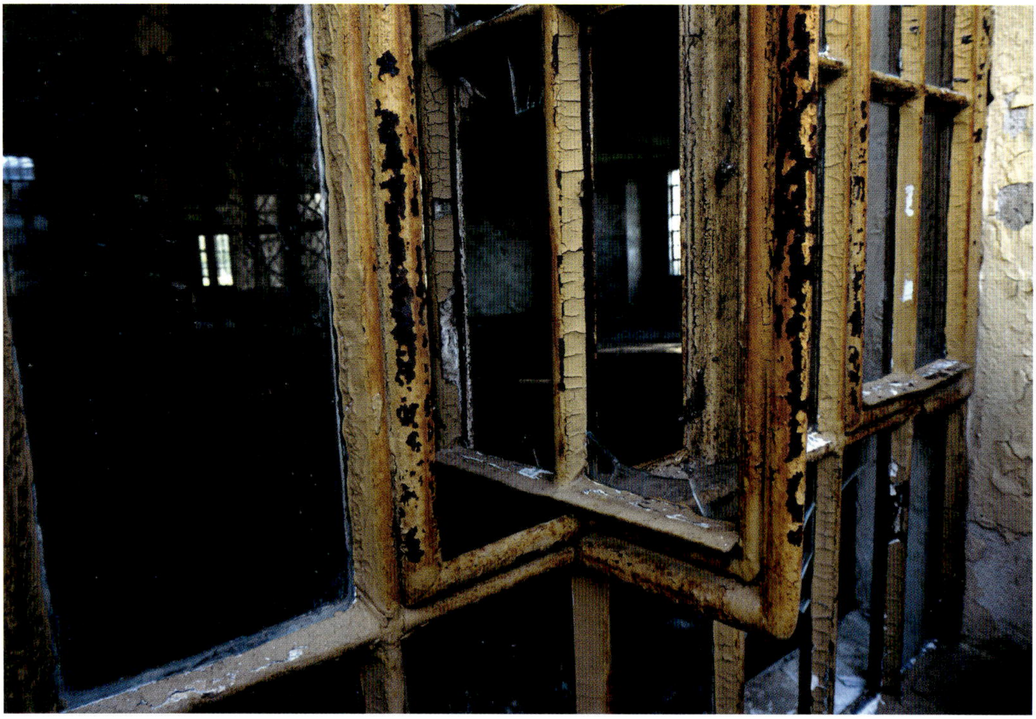

The windows' bright displays of orange paint now slowly fade as the years go by.

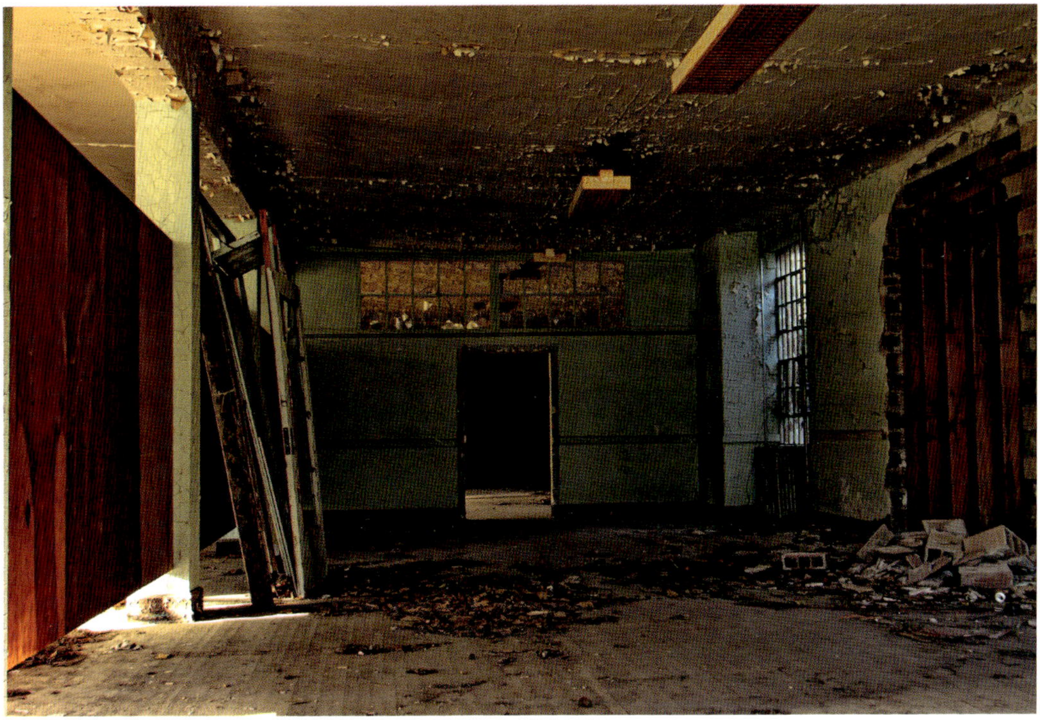

The Northern Hospital cafeteria was able to fit 400 people, which was shared by both the men and women's separate wards.

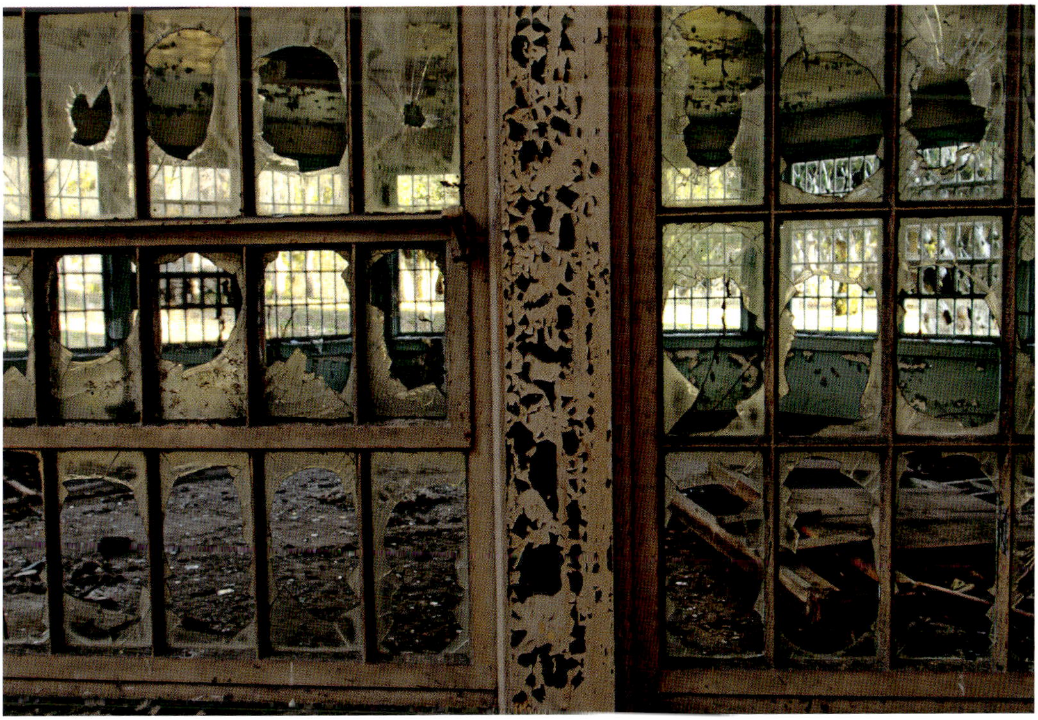

Unknown broken structures can be found throughout the buildings.

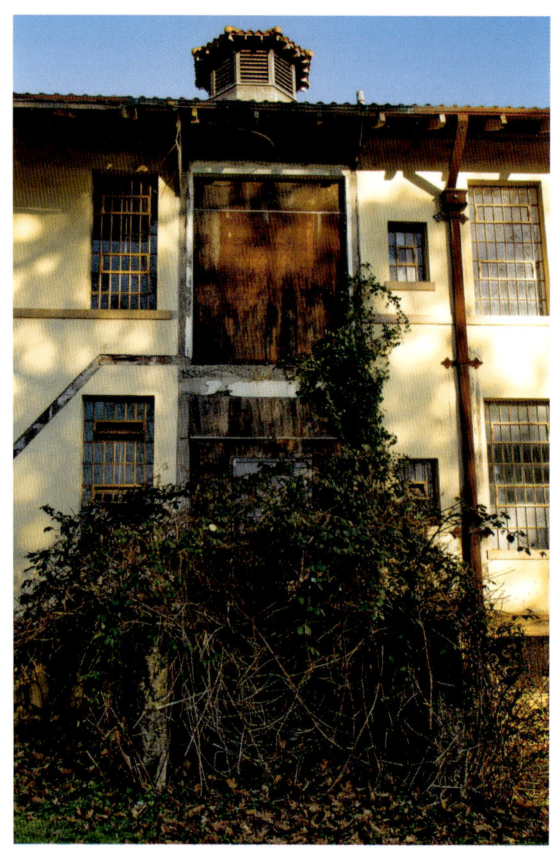

*Left:* The main hospital was built in 1912 and housed the hospital's switchboard.

*Below:* In its peak, Northern Hospital housed more than 2,500 patients, medical staff, and facility grounds keepers.

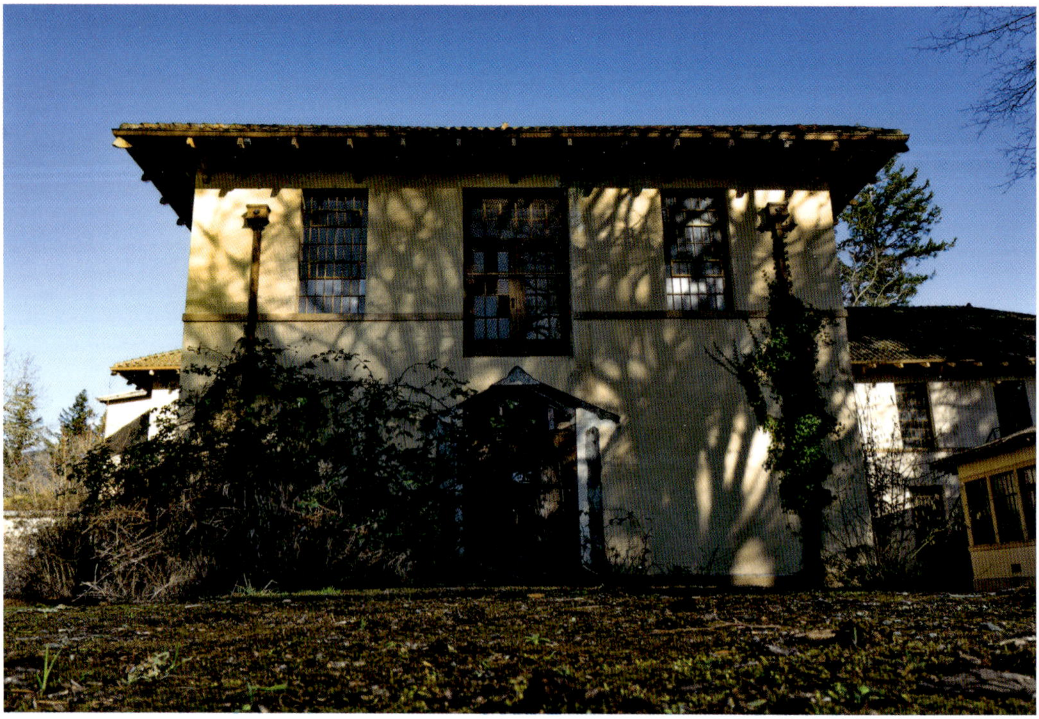

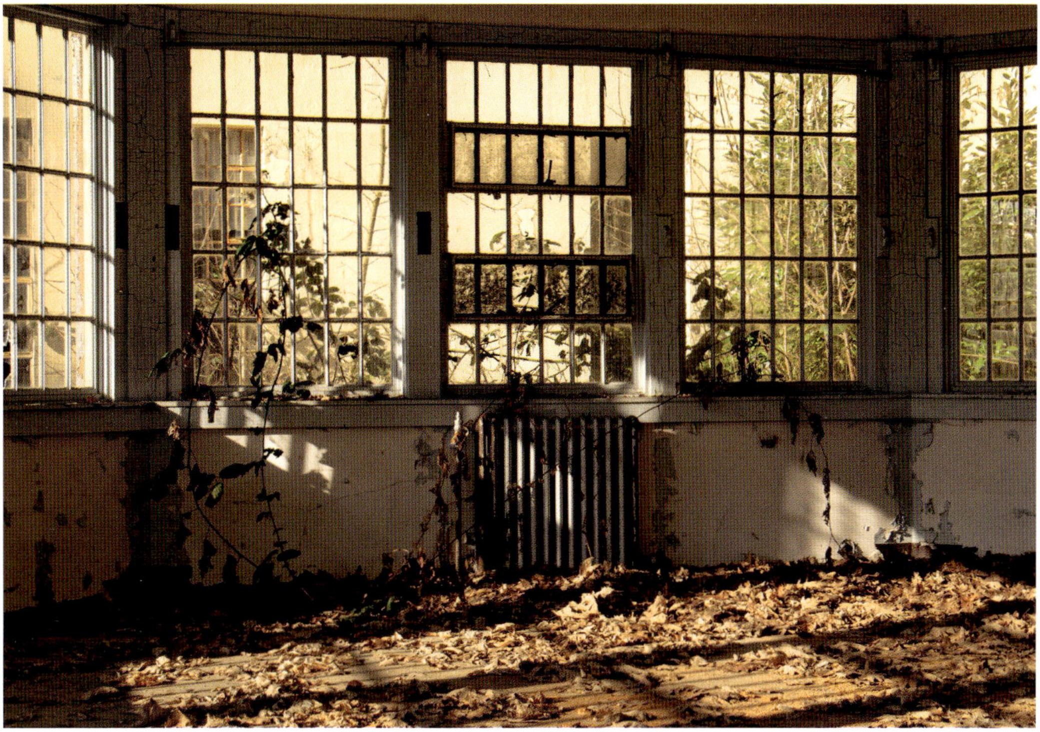

Beauty in the breakdown.

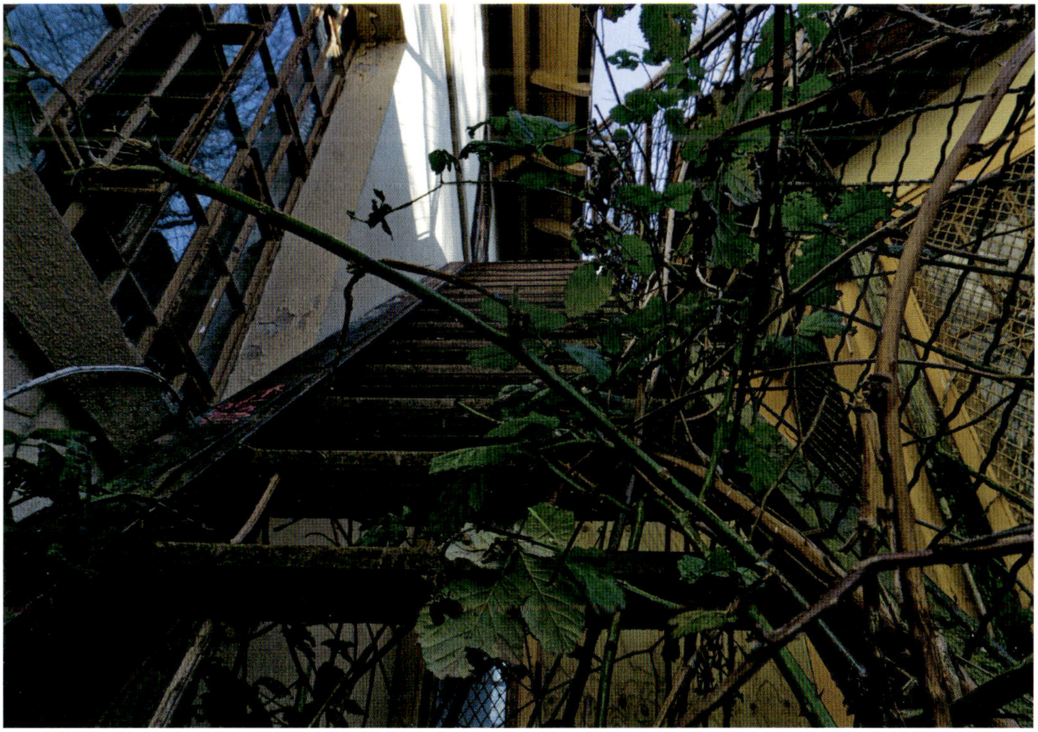

Thorns can be found in areas that are discouraged to enter.

# 2

# DEVIL'S TOWER

Formerly known as Baker, Washington, a town that sits along North Cascades Highway, it was not a point of destination until first settled in 1890. Many prospectors originally came to these lands with the promise of gold mines situated in the North Cascade Mountains. While many abandoned these hopes and dreams, leaving much disappointed, others that settled adapted to the lifestyle and claimed the land as their own. The land still sits perfectly situated today, southwest along the 150-mile-long Skagit River. The wildly flowing river runs through approximately 4,500 feet of elevation from the Cascade Range into the Puget Sound. Once explored, the land became perfect for agriculture, logging, mining, suburban, and residential development. It was only a matter of time before the area became an ideal resource for hydroelectric dams to supply electricity to not only the area but Seattle's city district as well.

Two neighboring towns became well known in these parts for each having their own cement-manufacturing industries, as the area had an unlimited supply of limestone deposits. Washington Portland Cement Company was built in 1905 in what was known as "Cement City." Superior Portland Cement Building opened its doors in Baker 1908. By 1909, both the towns decided to merge as it was what was best for both, and they agreed on a new name that was more fitting: Concrete, Washington. A few years would pass and eventually both cement industries would also merge. By 1923, the Superior Portland Cement Building became the largest Portland cement manufacturer in the country.

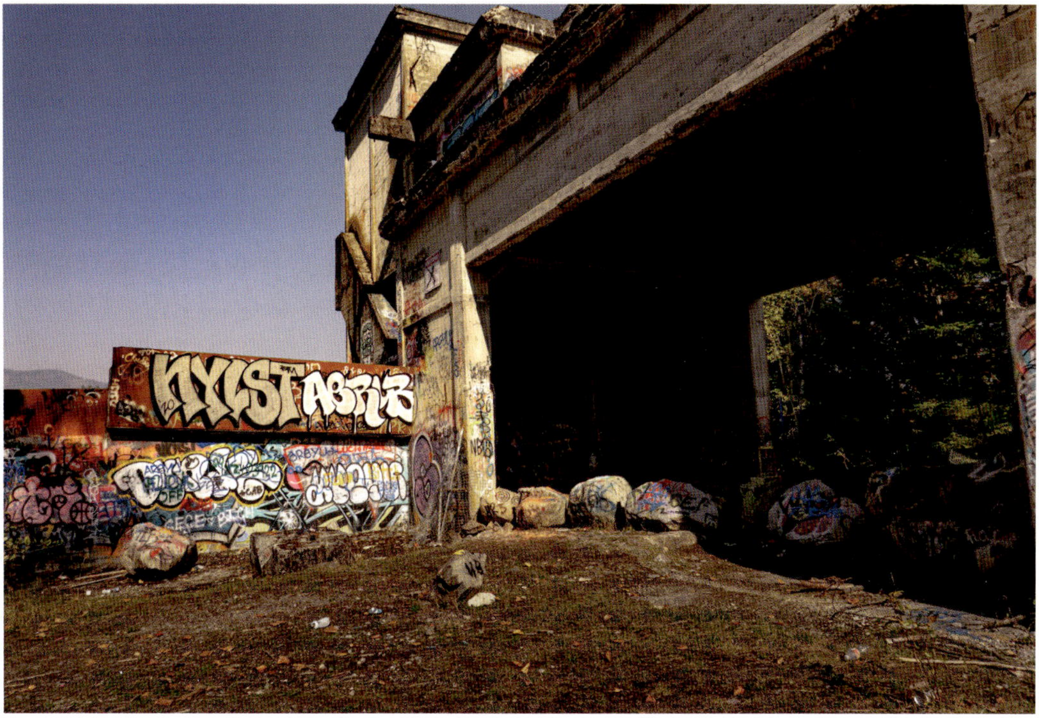

A railroad used to run through this entryway 2 miles into the quarry.

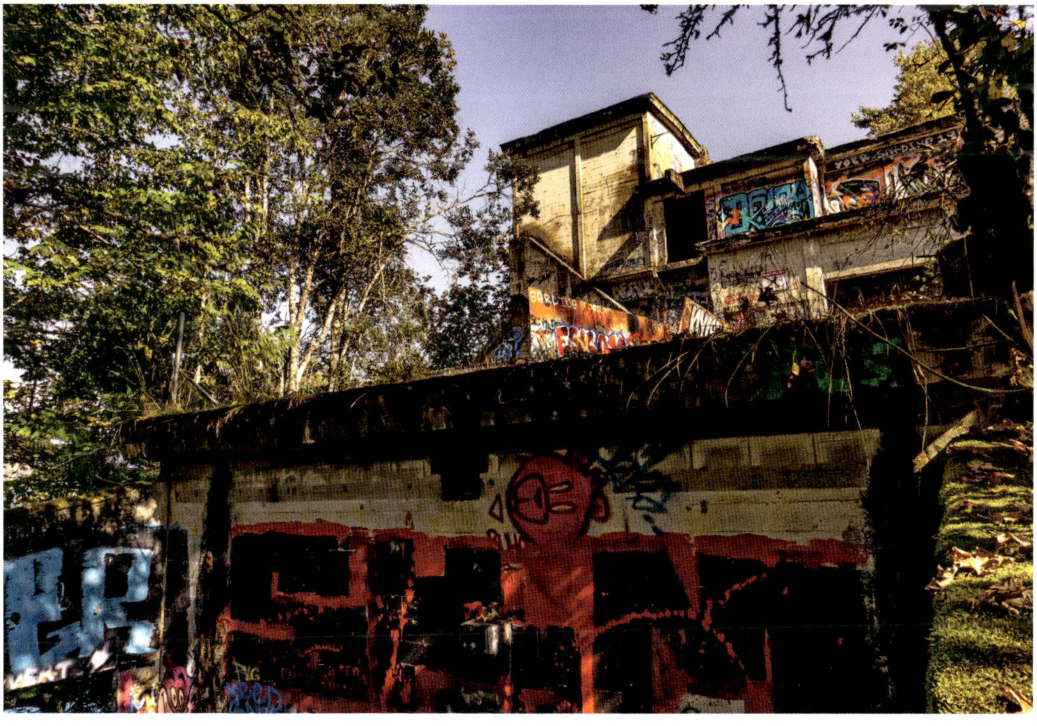

The structure itself is about eight flights high, with each level offering a different purpose to the construction of Portland Cement.

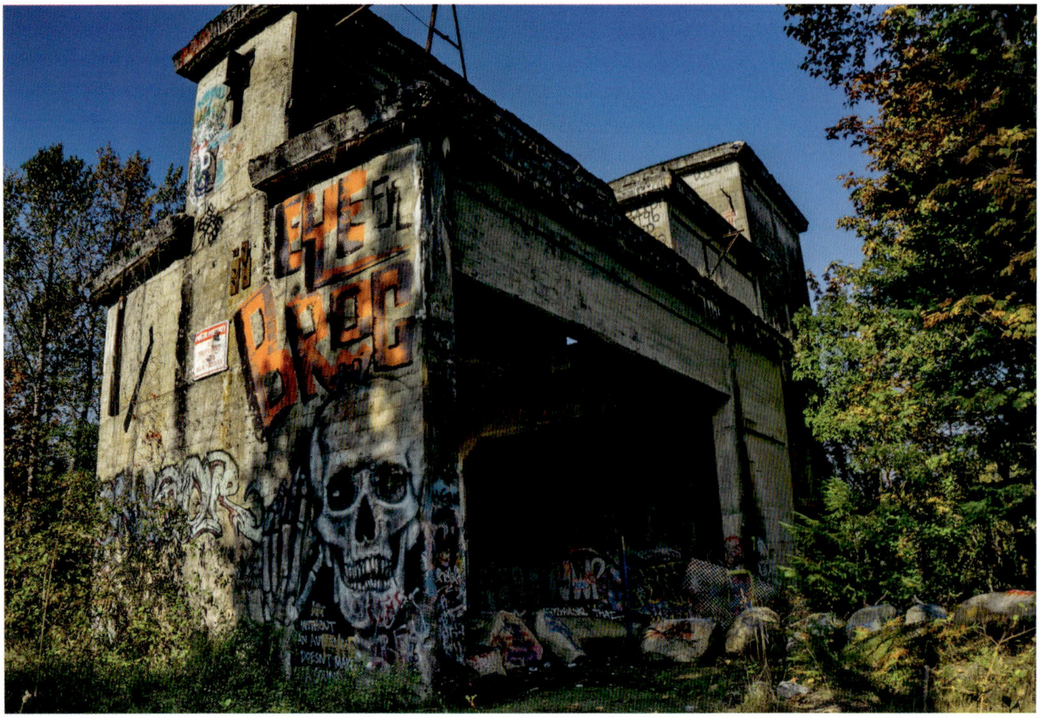

The crusher is where rocks would get transported from the quarry and the process of breaking down the limestone would begin.

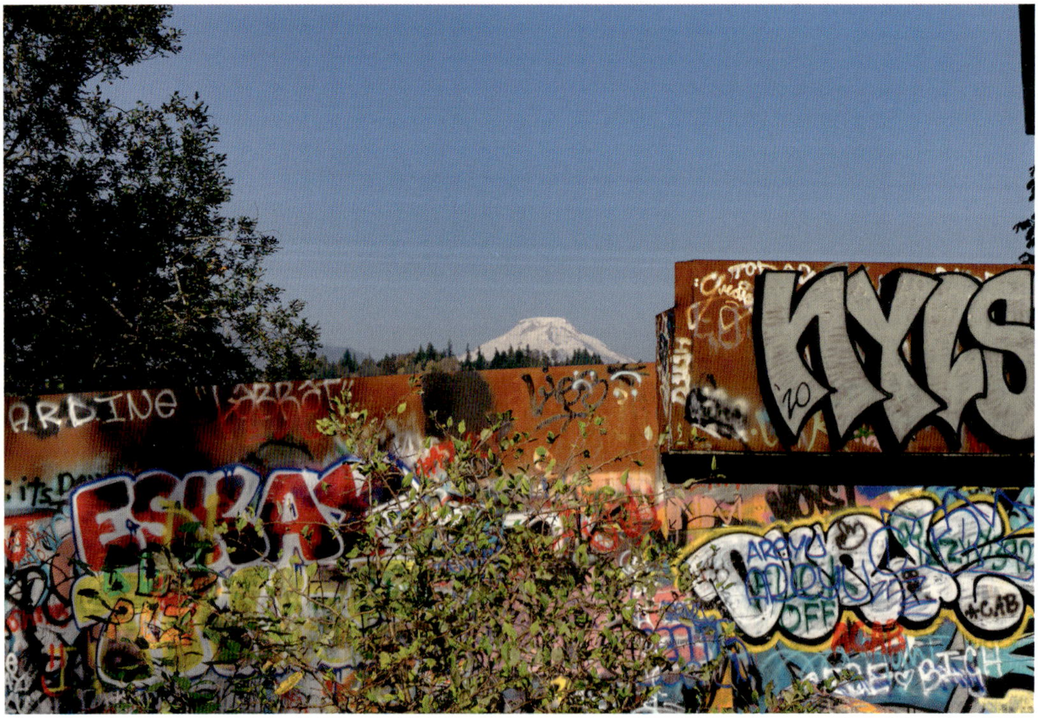

Netting and vines ran along the structure, with pipes hanging midair.

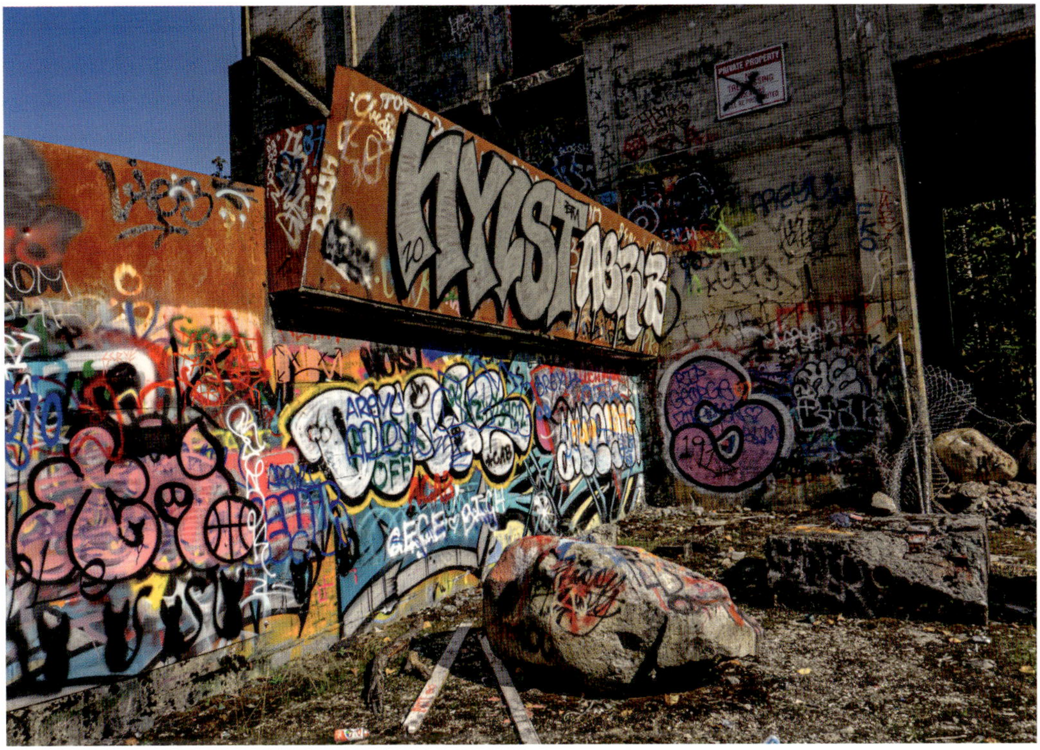

A popular spot among local kids, boulders are placed in areas to be avoided.

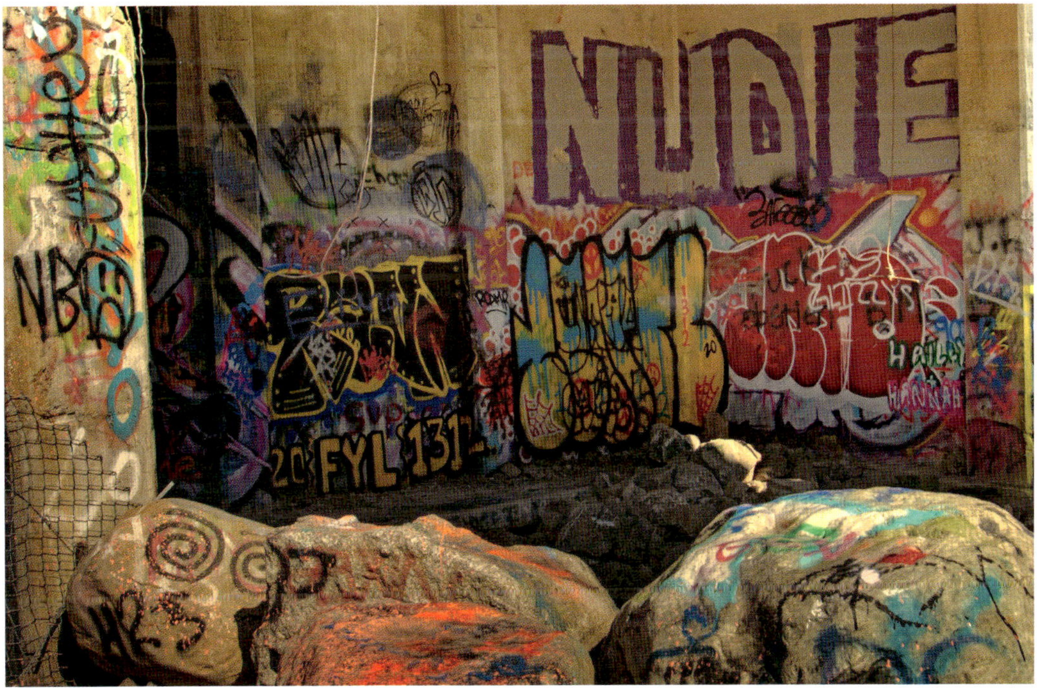

An area blocked off to avoid people getting hurt is ironically the same area where boulders would begin to get cru3hed.

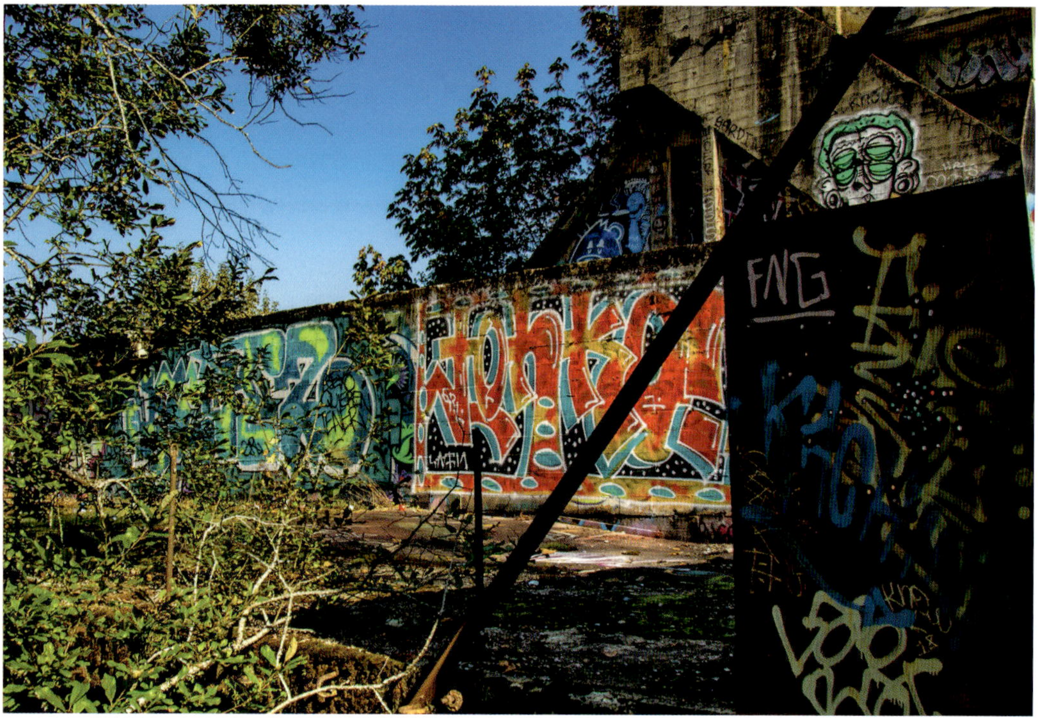

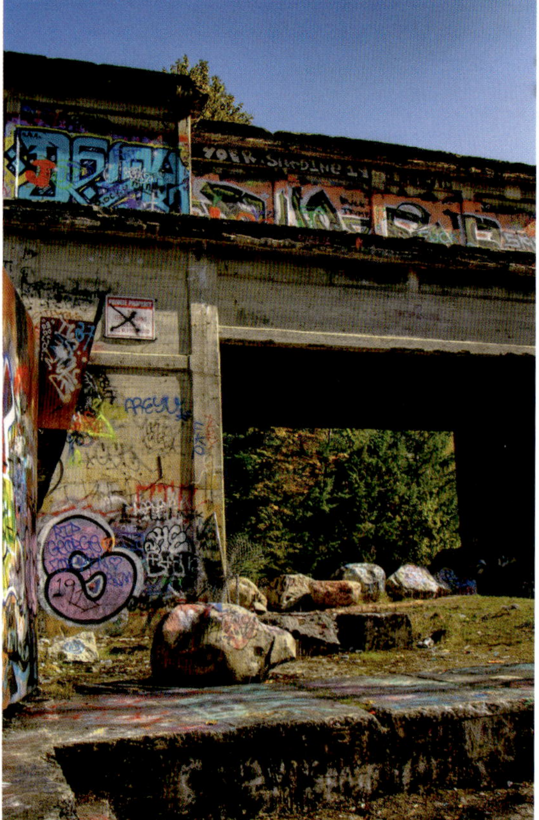

*Above:* One of the exterior ground level views on the property.

*Left:* The facility serviced the many dams in the area.

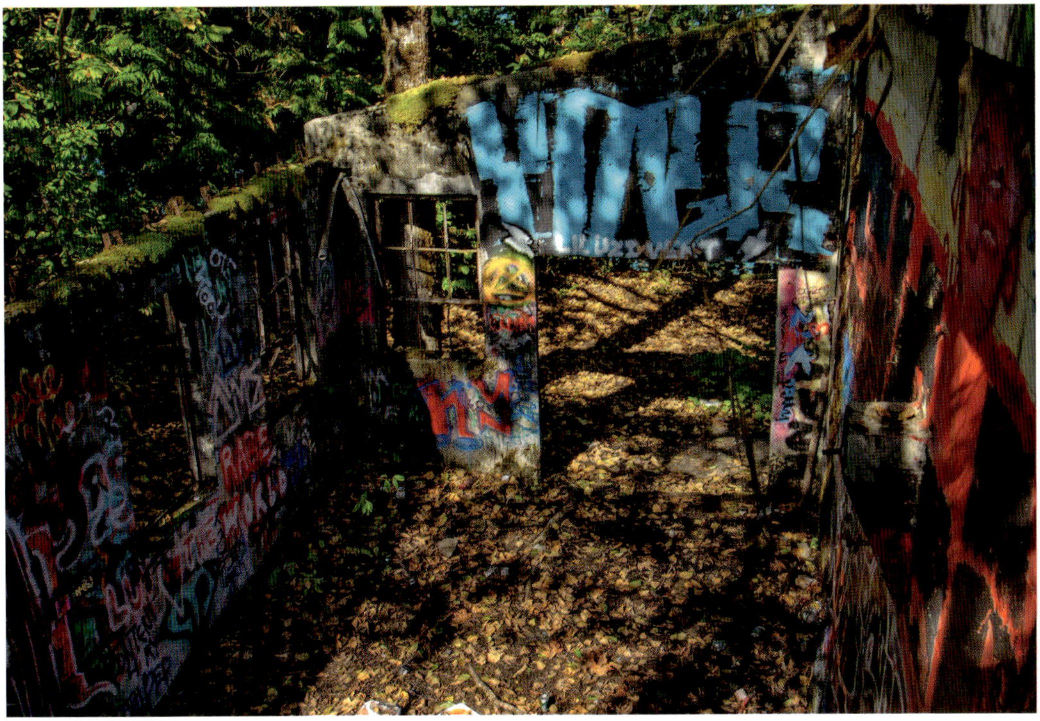

If you retrace your steps and take a lower path, you will end up in lower facilities of the building that were hidden originally.

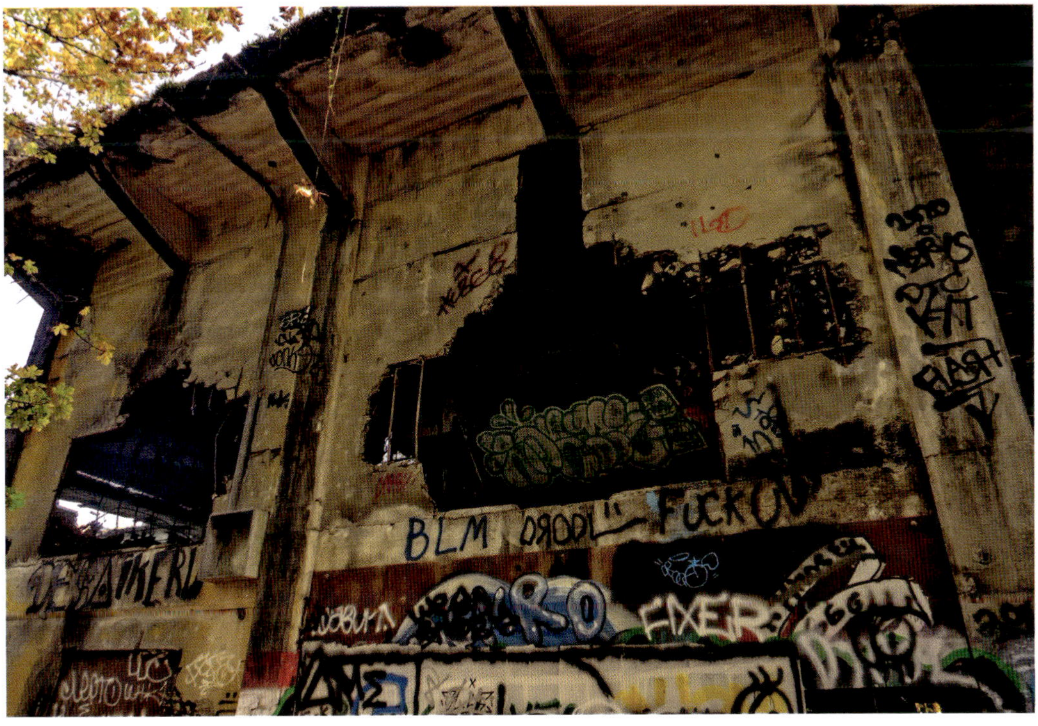

Machinery was removed from the buildings upon announcing their close, and only holes remain.

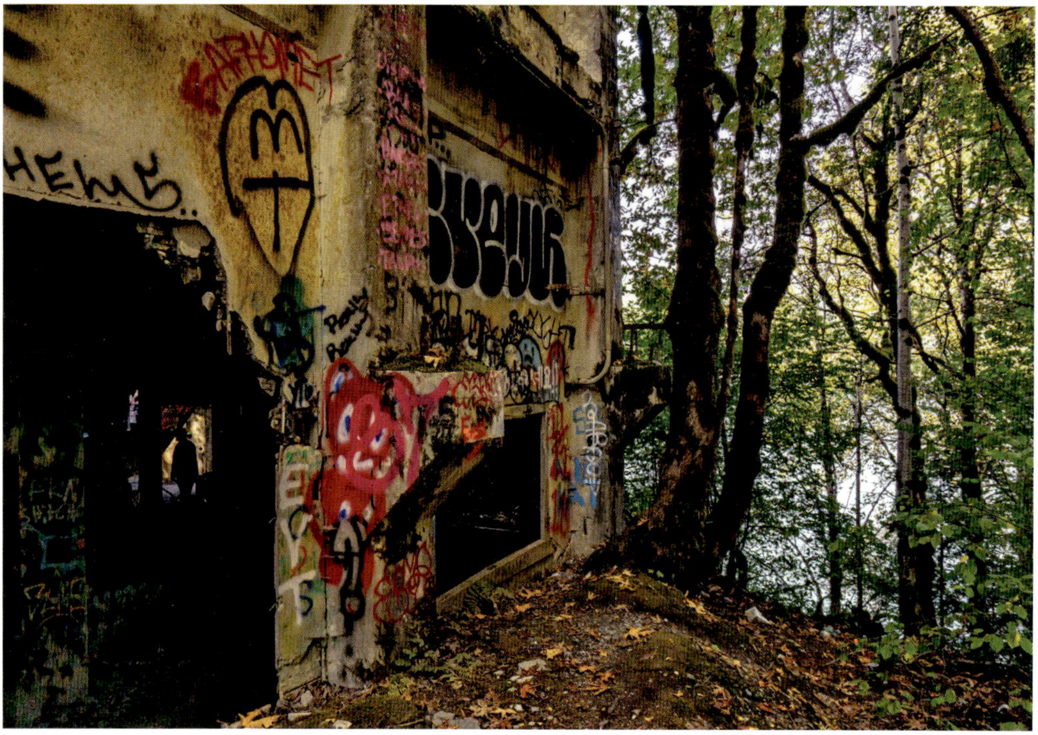

The factory sits along Lake Shannon, which formed from the creation of Lower Baker Dam.

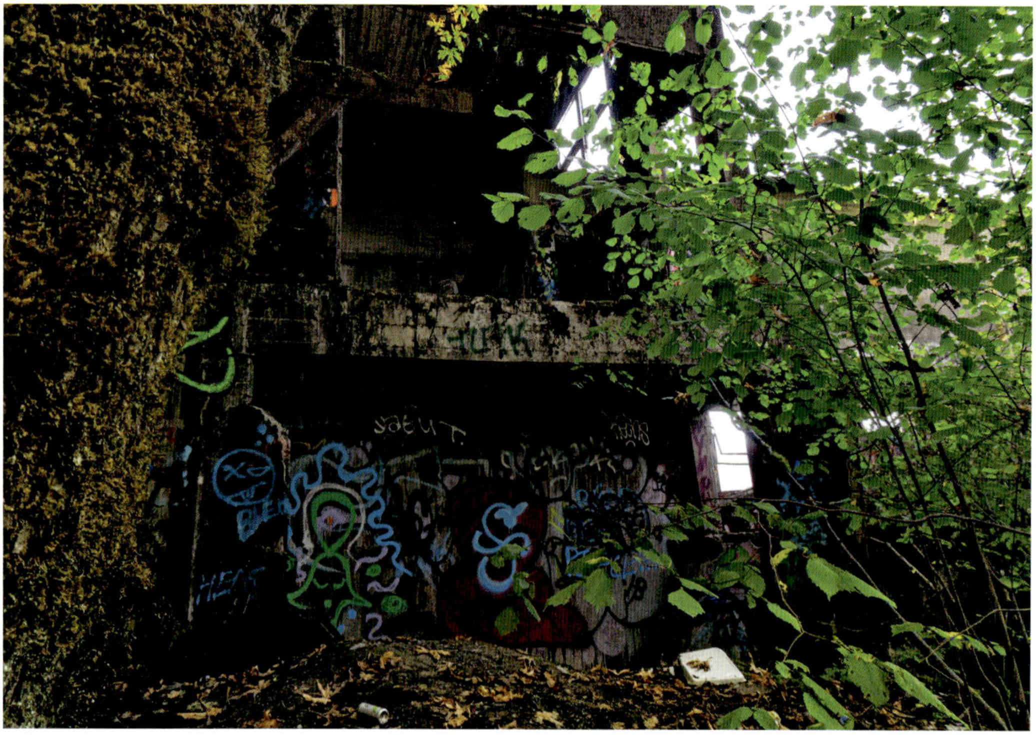

Along the back side of the factory, one will find lower levels to different entryways to the structure.

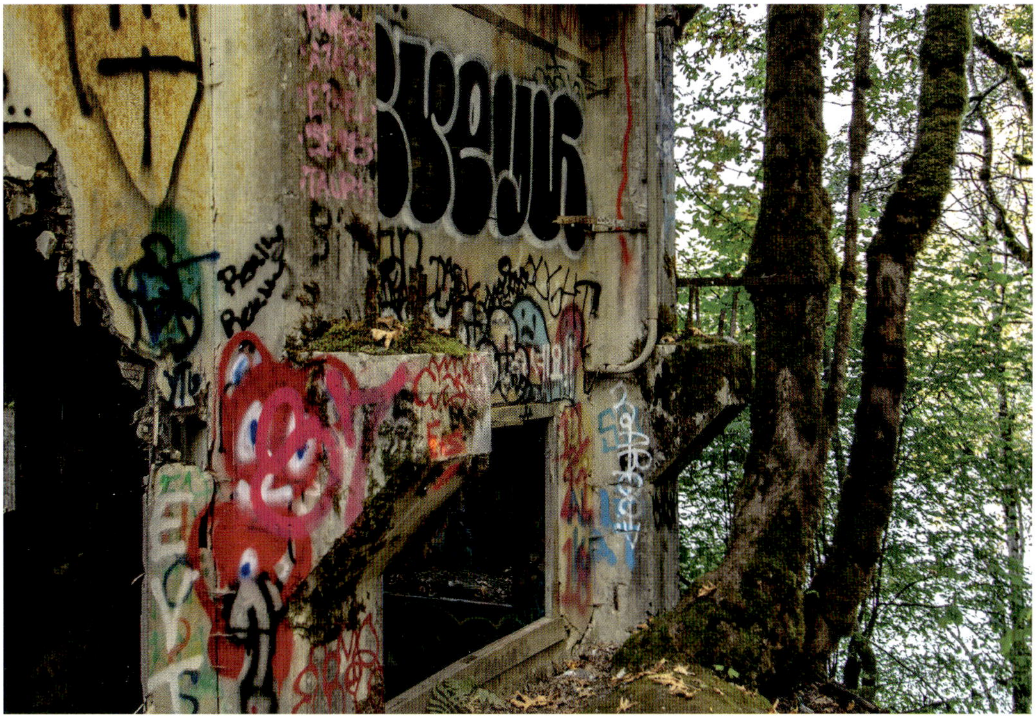

*Above:* The holes along the south side appear to be also used for different machinery, as every area had a different purpose.

*Right:* Each room was designed to flow materials smoothly through the process intentionally.

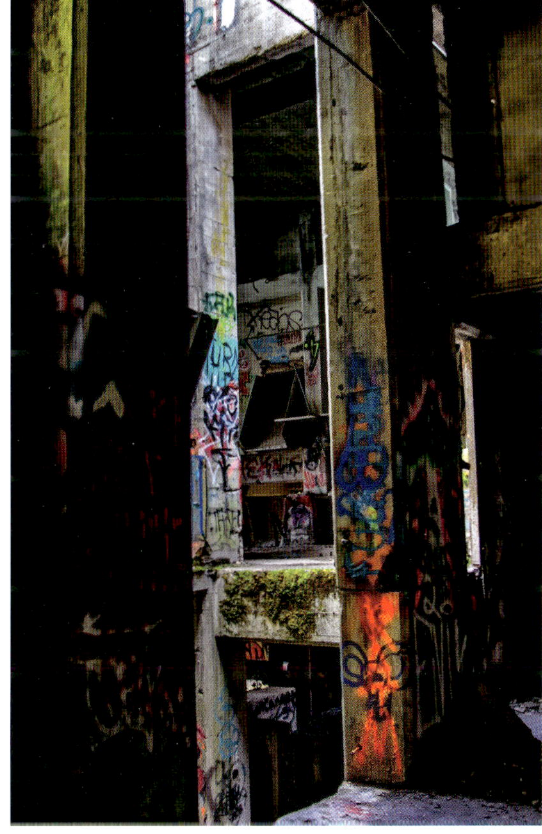

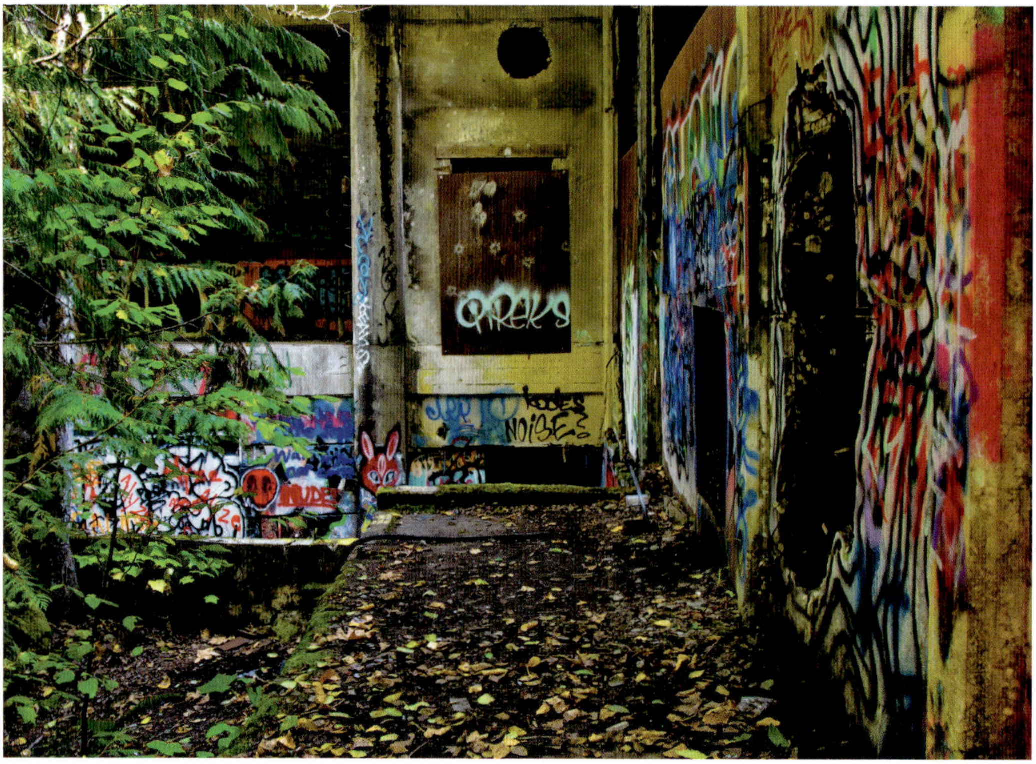

Trees have begun to grow through the building structure.

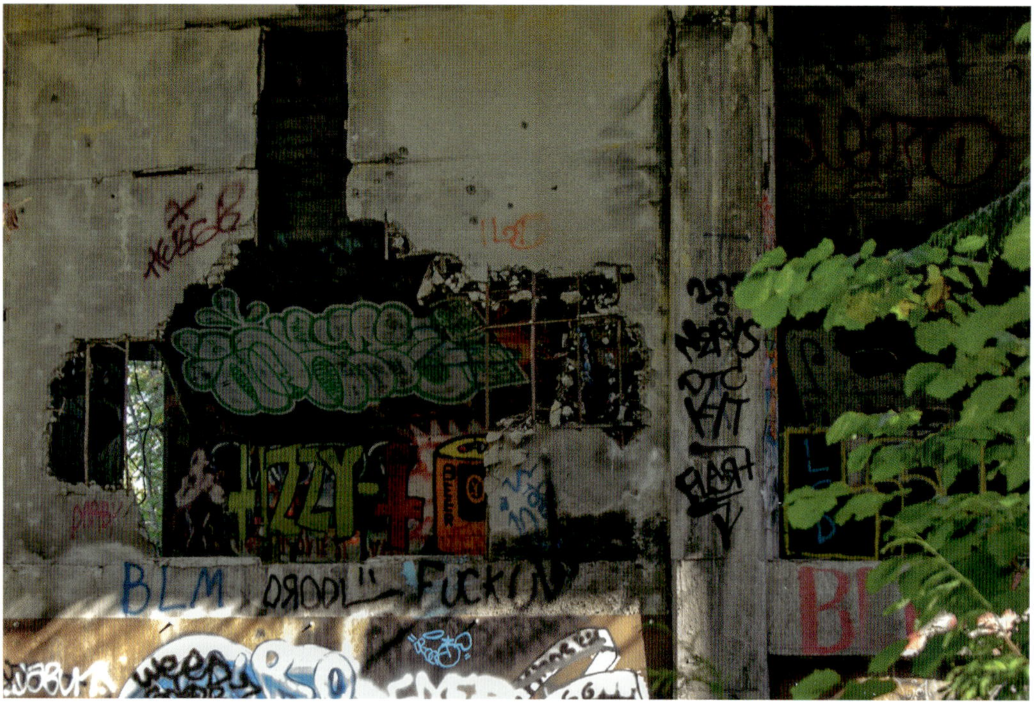

The building has been owned by many owners; the last was Lone Star Company.

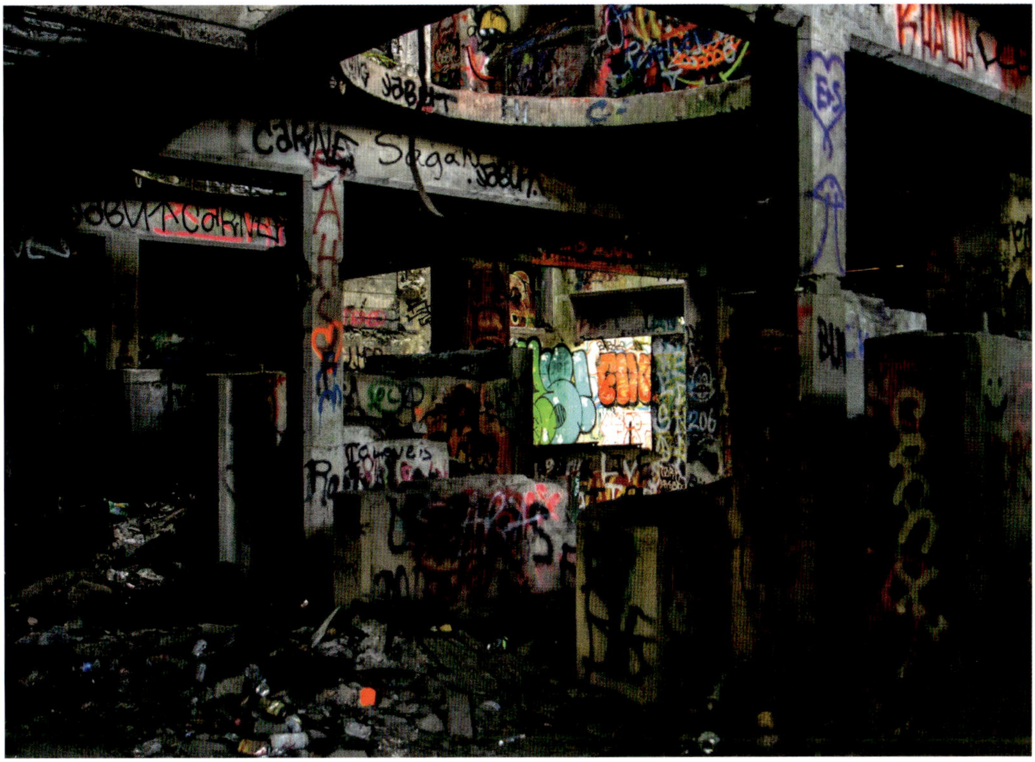

*Above:* The basement had very low visible light and not much room for footwork with all the concrete and beer cans strewn everywhere.

*Right:* Windows now busted and rusted over.

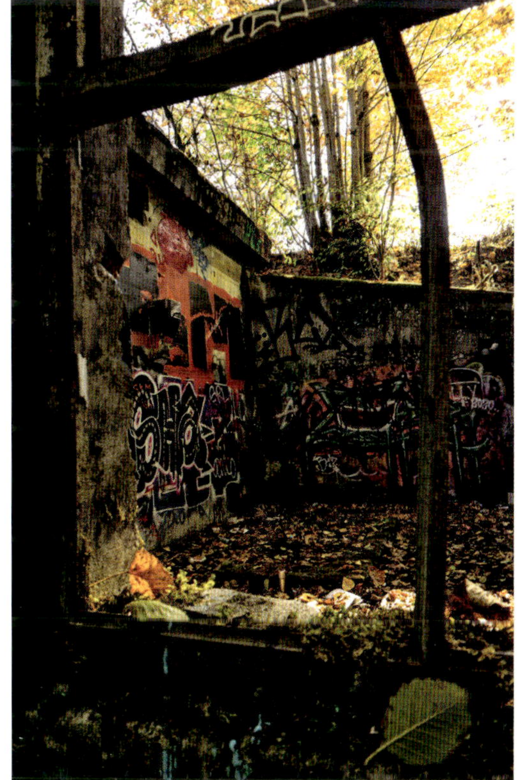

It was found that Superior Portland Cement Building helped develop nearby hydropower dam constructions of Lower Baker Dam, as well as the Skagit River Hydroelectric Project, which consisted of Gorge Dam, Diablo Dam, and Ross Dam. Gorge's construction began in 1921 and power was first delivered to Seattle in 1924. The Lower Baker Dam was completed in 1925 as the highest hydroelectric dam in the world at that time and formed Lake Shannon. In 1927, 5 miles upstream from Gorge, Diablo's construction began; it was completed in 1930. At that time, Diablo was the tallest dam in the world at 389 feet. Seattle had one of the larger power projects in the west by the time the dam delivered electricity in 1936. By 1937, construction began on Ross Dam, formerly known as Ruby Dam (this was changed due to the passing of James Delmage Ross, the superintendent of the Skagit River Project in 1939). This dam was developed in three stages, which at its final height was 540 feet. Gorge, Diablo, and Ross Dam generate enough power to supply about 20 percent of Seattle's electricity.

The Superior Portland Cement Company once started off with a capital stock of $10,000, later raising $525,000. They then purchased 7,500 acres of land and the former Center Furnace company that could convert raw materials like limestone and charcoal and turn them into iron, providing them with a great start to their soon-to-be-booming business. The property looks out over the east bank of Lake Shannon with magnificent views of Mount Baker's snow cap, standing tall at 10,778 feet. The area is situated nestled right between Mount Baker-Snoqualmie National Forest and North Cascades National Park, surrounded by wildlife and nature on all sides. The site contained a quarry with a 2-mile railway between it and the site, a crusher building that railway ran through, bunker for loading railroad cars, coal plant, machine shop, pipe shop, carpenter shop, belt shop, welding shop, storage building, concrete pressure testing lab, cement kilns, clay converter, silos, and more.

As the years went by, the company faced unprecedented lack of rainfalls, which in turn created power shortages and the business went through many changes of ownership.

By 1967, the Lone Star Cement Corporation, the final owners of the facility, announced its gradual closing of all operations. First the quarry was deactivated, then the kilns, the grinding, then storage and shipping would end once all orders were shipped. Lone Star stated it cost more money to maintain the plant with operating costs so steep and equipment so out of date; it was not economically feasible to keep the operation open. At one time, this company was what put Concrete on the map and now the building has become a relic, now owned by the city of Concrete, Washington. The 2012 census provides the city's population has decreased more than 50 percent to 705 people since the merging of the two cities.

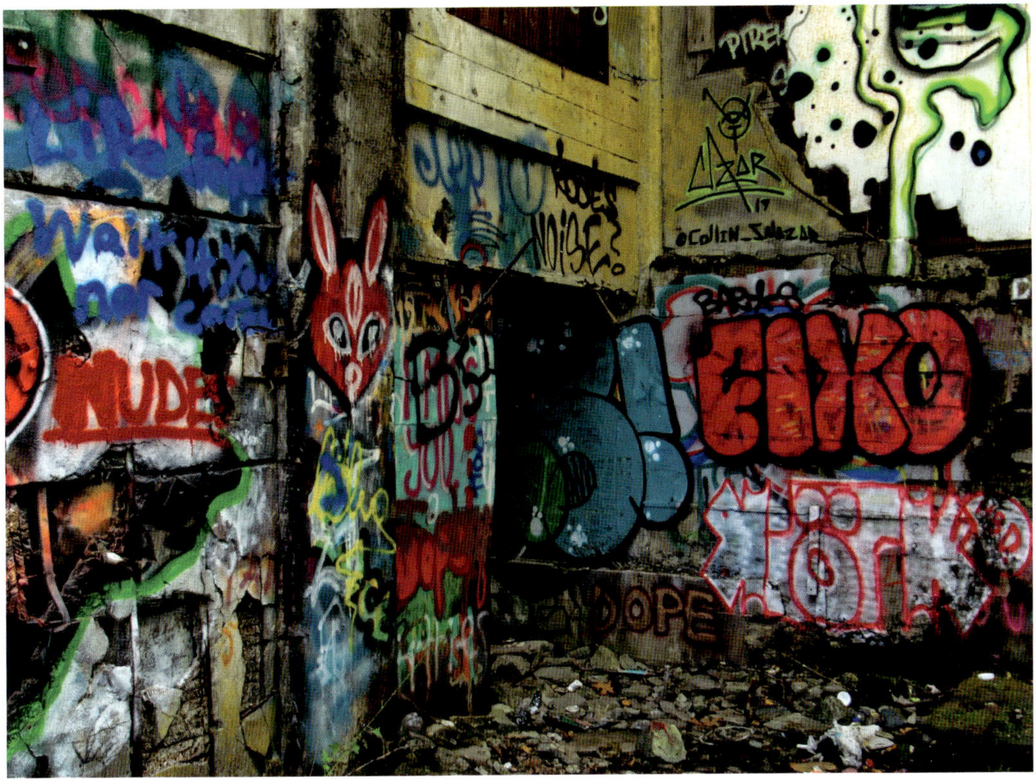

*Above:* Broken glass and rocks line the floor level of the factory, graffiti covered almost every reachable inch of wall.

*Right:* The factory was founded by those on the quest for gold, who settled for limestone deposits instead.

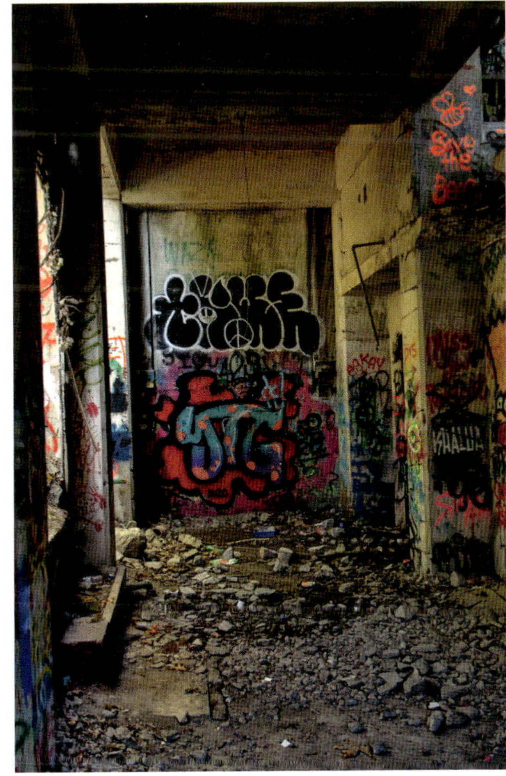

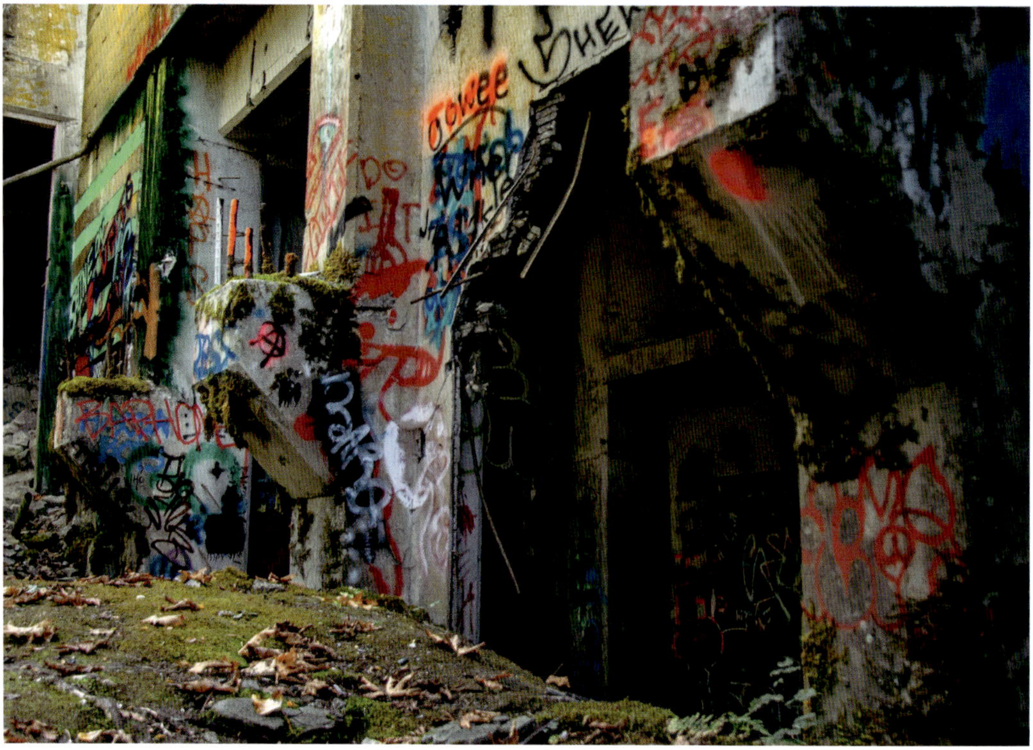

The area prior to becoming Concrete, was known as Baker, Cement City, and a small neighborhood called Superior.

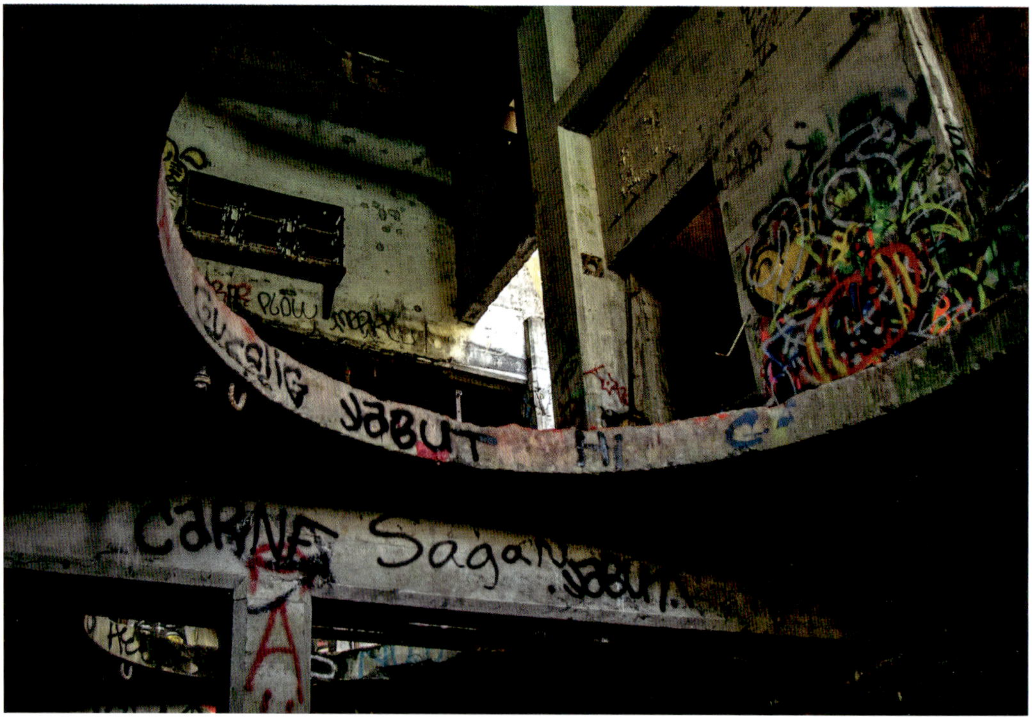

Views upward from the basement.

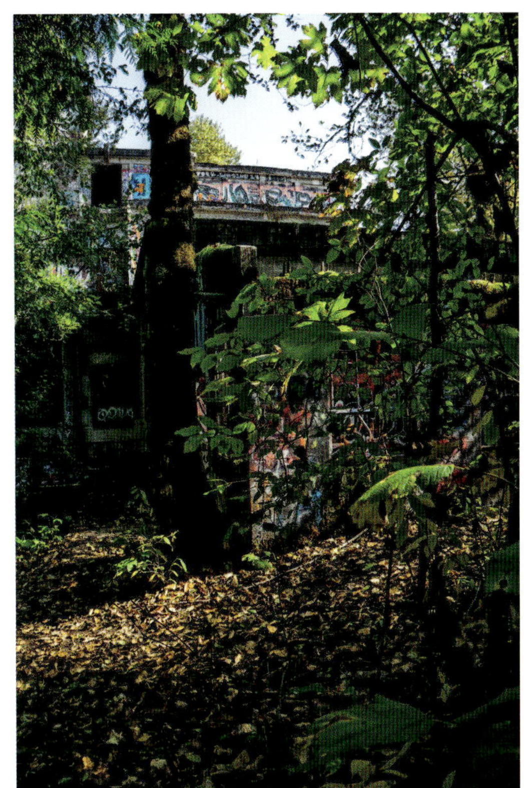

*Right:* The structure is built into the hillside sitting next to Lake Shannon; this once-entryway bared no trees shading it from the public's eye.

*Below:* Both cement factories in Concrete, Superior Portland Cement Company and Washington Portland Cement Company, joined to be known as Superior Portland Cement Company.

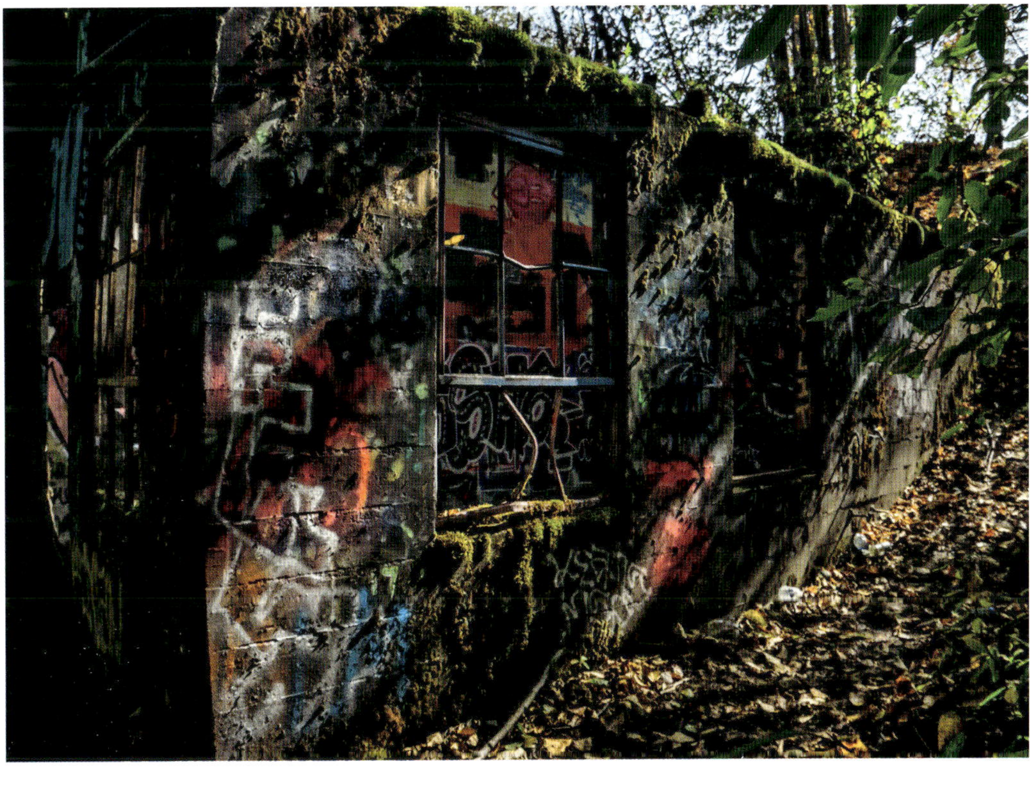

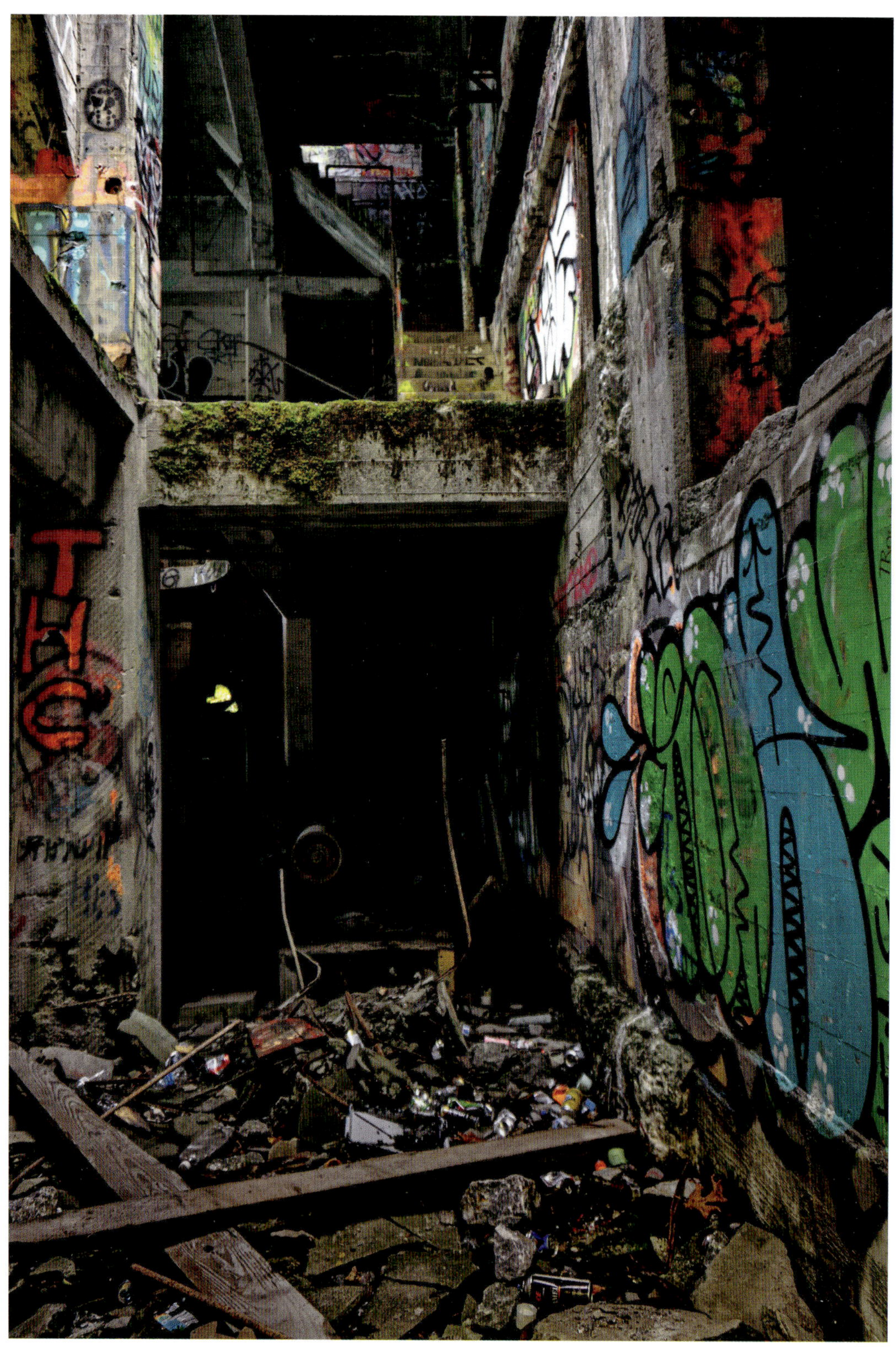


Nature has welcomed the building as its own, bringing weeds and moss to life.

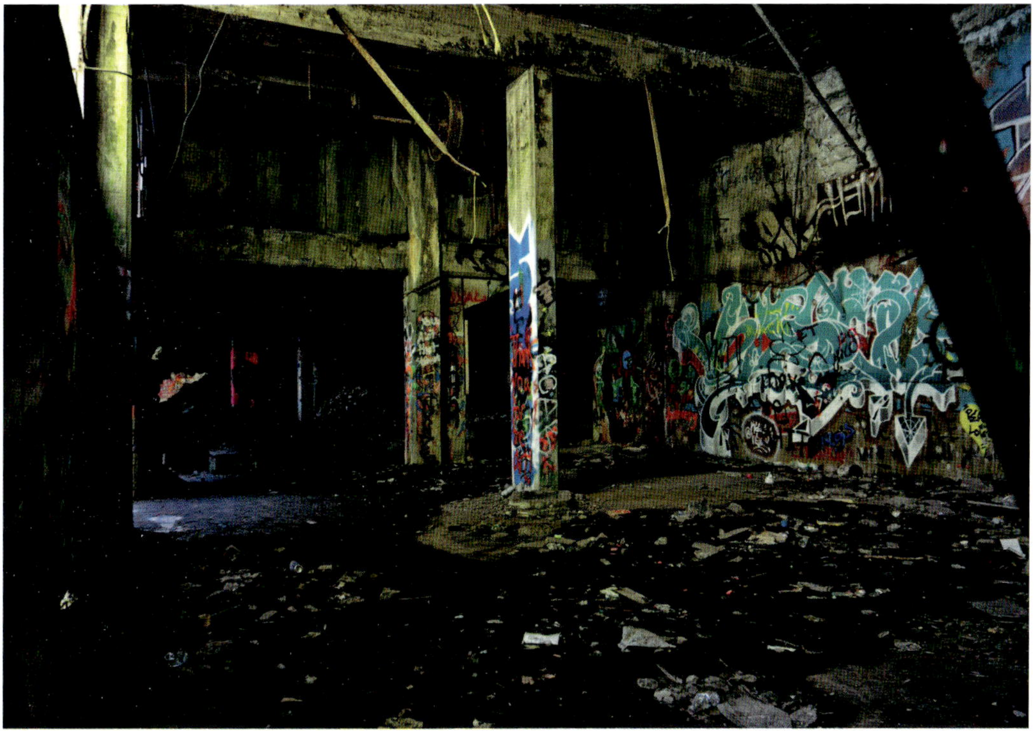

Big open areas show where cement would be reaching its final stages of production near the bottom of the building.

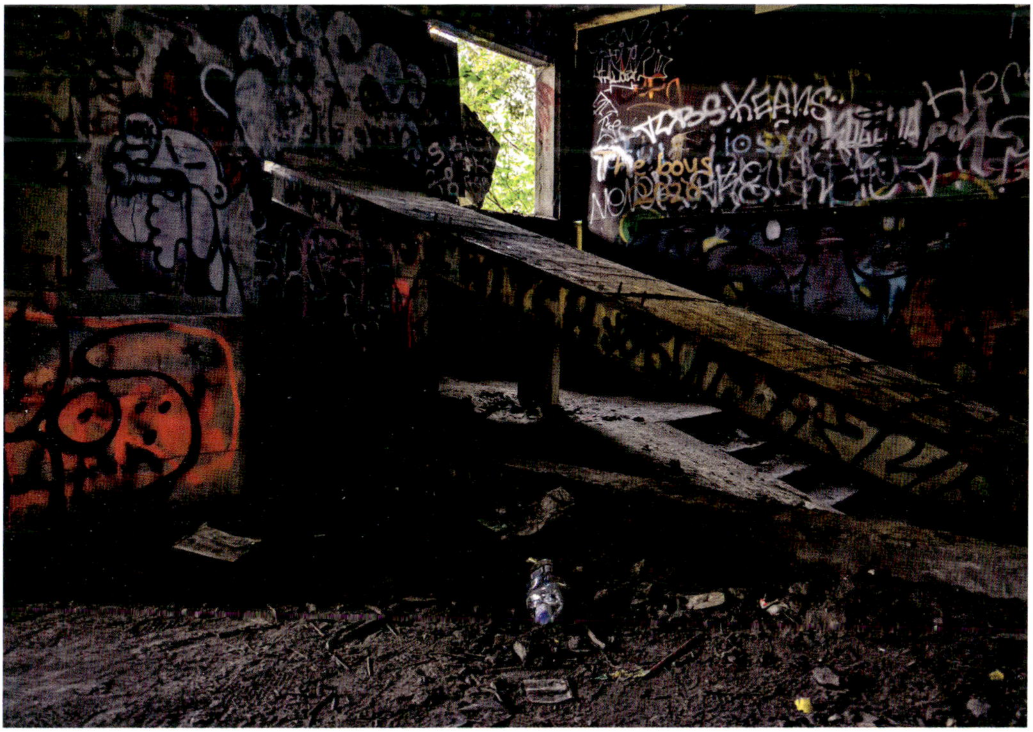

Ramps for production still can be found along the basement levels.

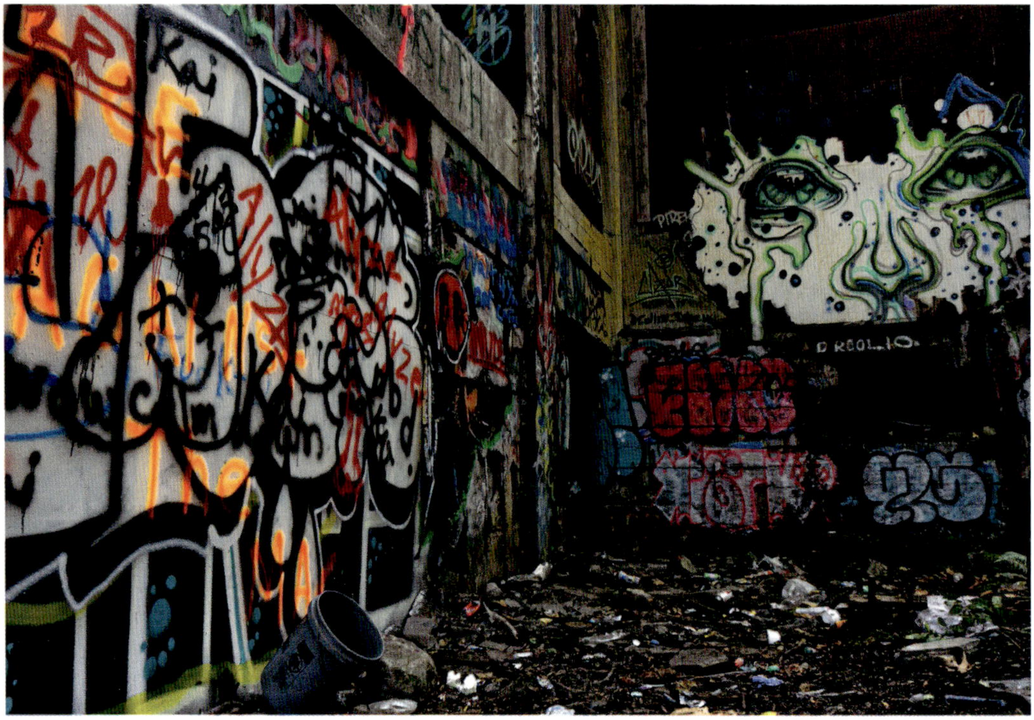

Concrete's most historic business, which it was known for, was its cement industry.

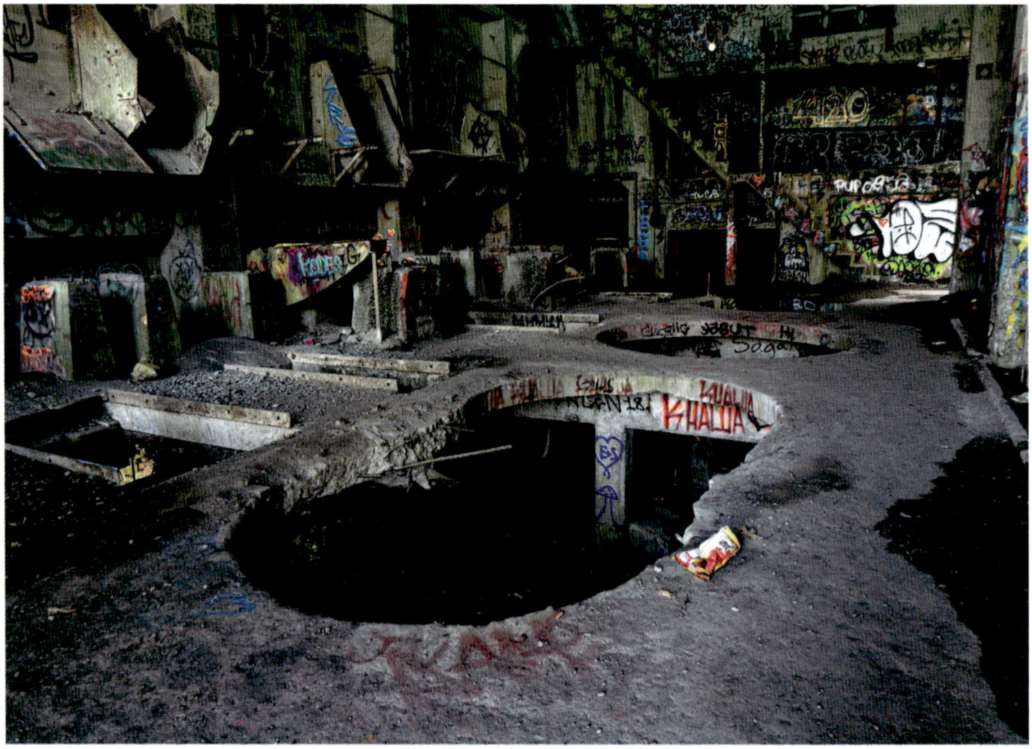

No one actually knows how Devil's Tower got its name, but it definitely is spooky.

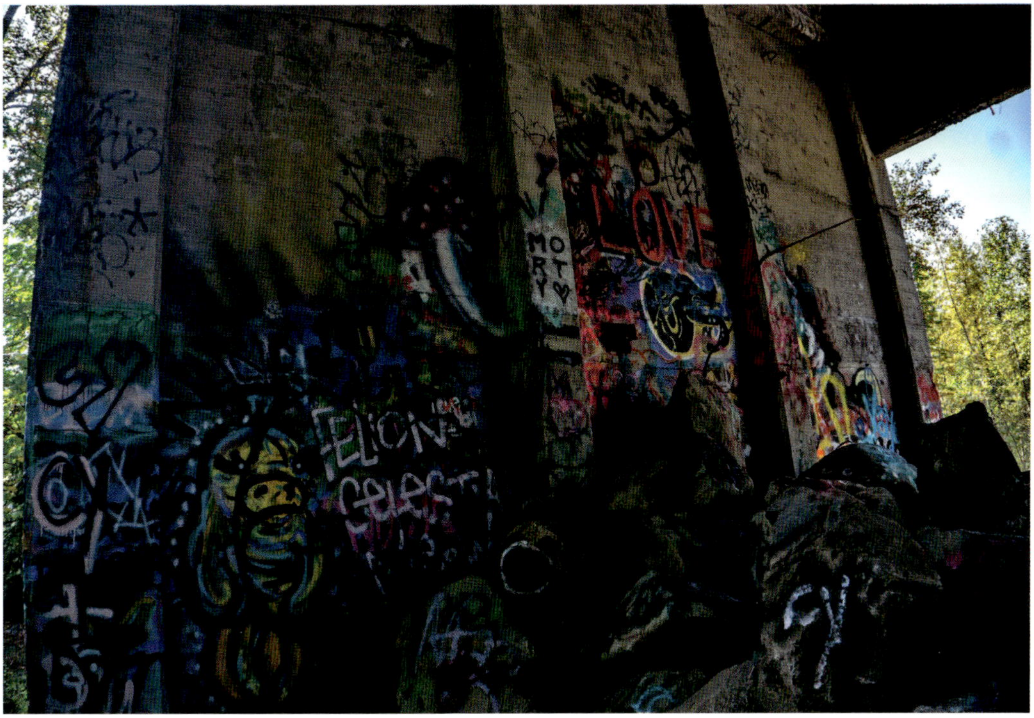

A different perspective of the rock crusher where rocks would get transported from the quarry.

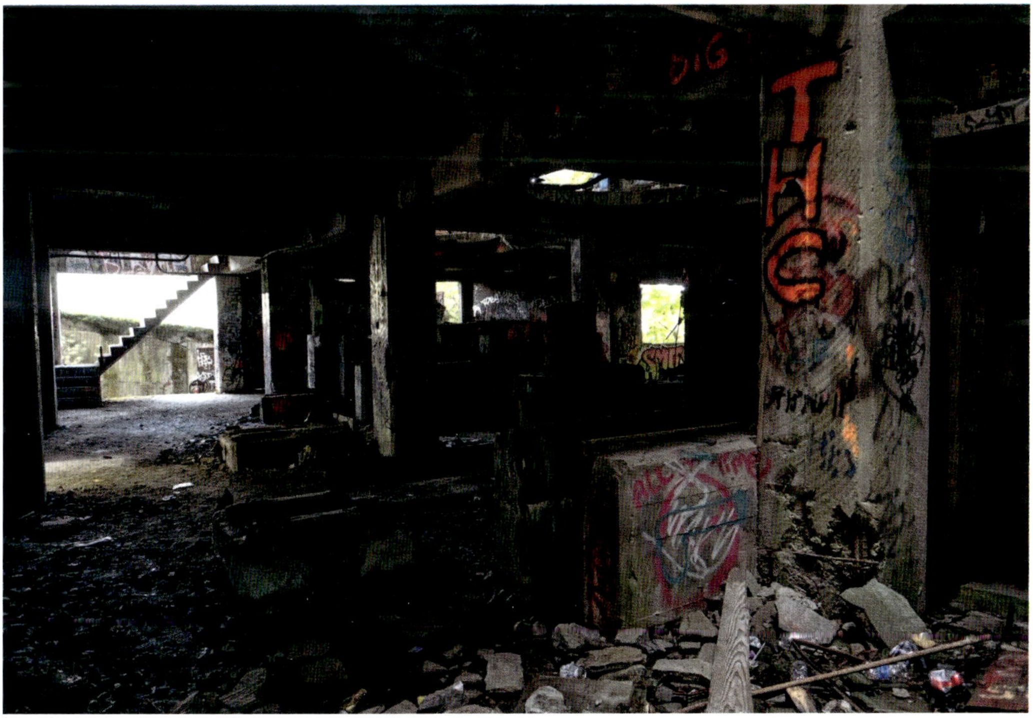

By 1923, Superior Portland Cement Company was the largest Portland cement manufactured in the country at that tlme.

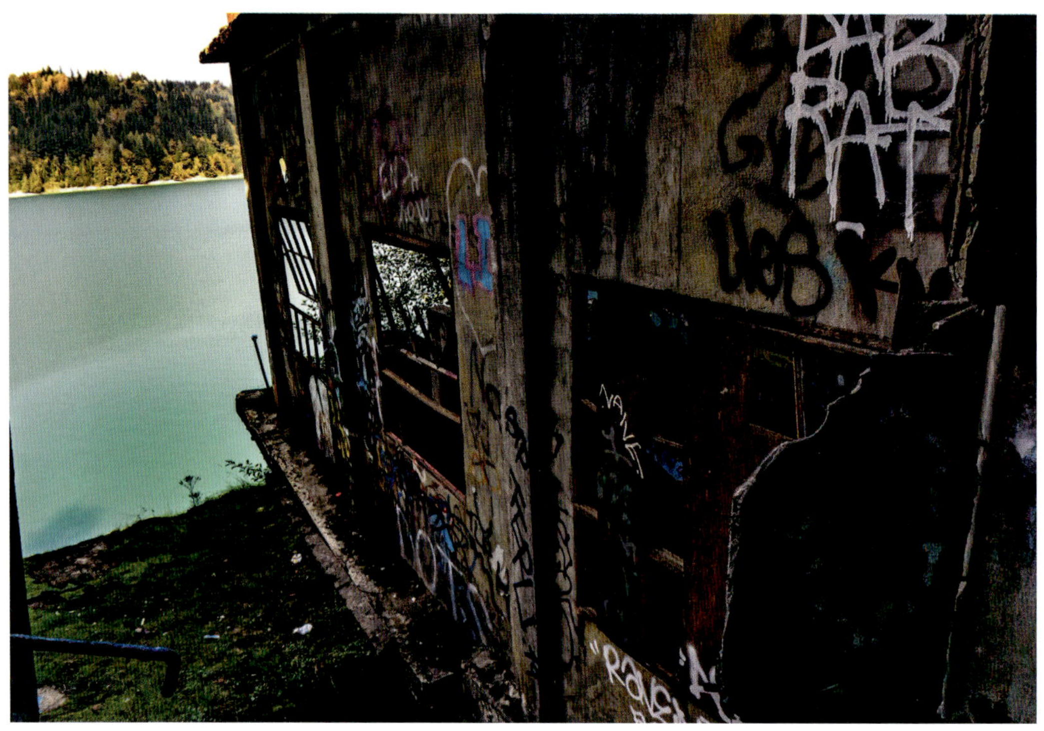

Lake Shannon offered a beautiful view to the abandoned playground.

The Skagit River Hydroelectric Project is said to approximate 92 percent of the electricity used in Seattle as of 2012. Concrete will always be known as regionally significant to the development of the Pacific Northwest. The cement factories played a major role in developing all of Concrete, numerous projects in Seattle's development, and major infrastructures throughout the North Cascades Area. Concrete now sits as a tiny quaint mountain town along the highway. The abandoned structures of what locals refer to as Devil's Tower still stand today, and they give one a friendly reminder of our yesteryears.

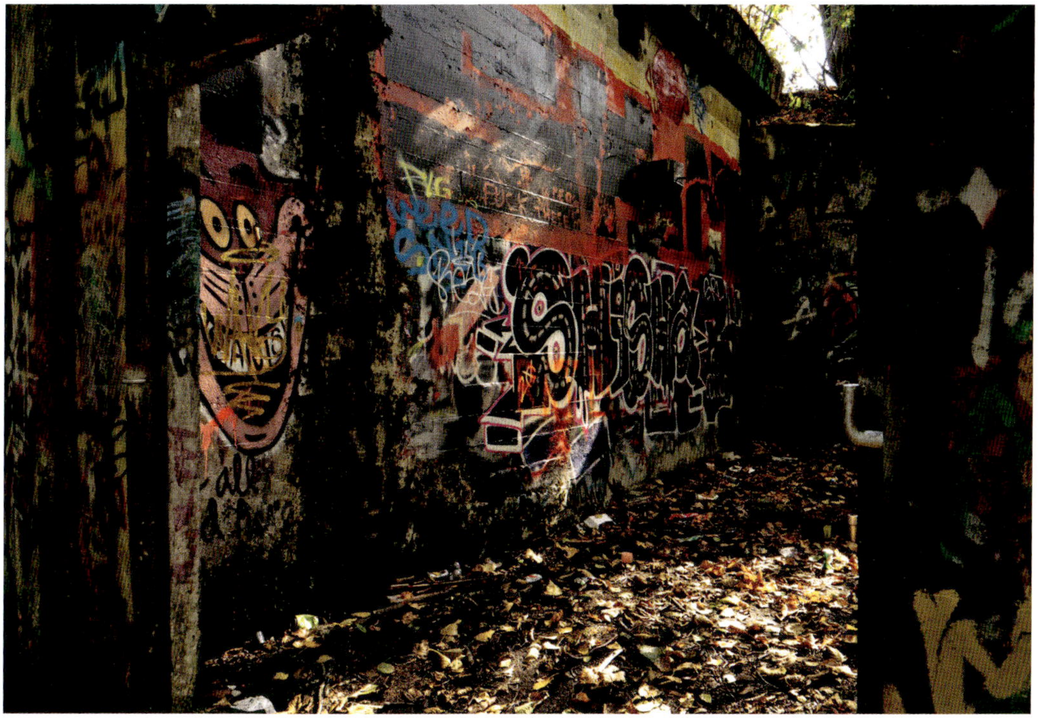

*Above:* Nature always finds a way.

*Right:* Steep staircases lined the insides of the facility, each level steeper than the last with no railing on site.

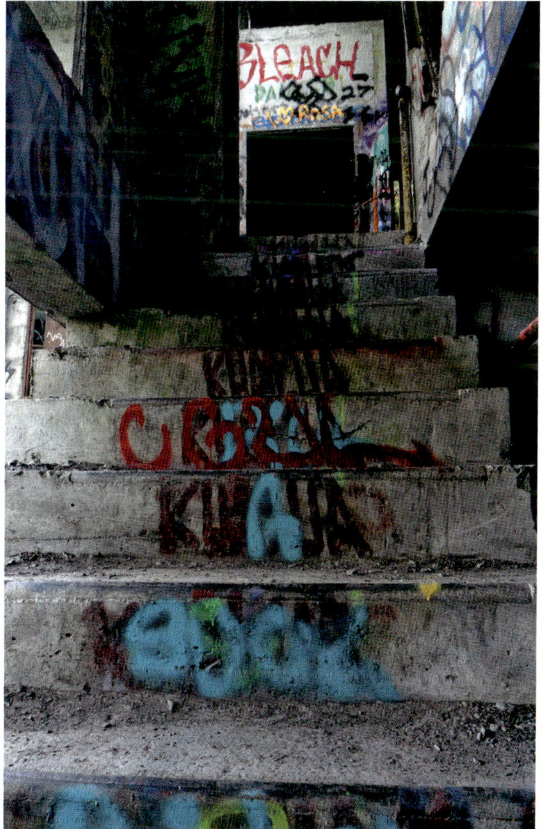

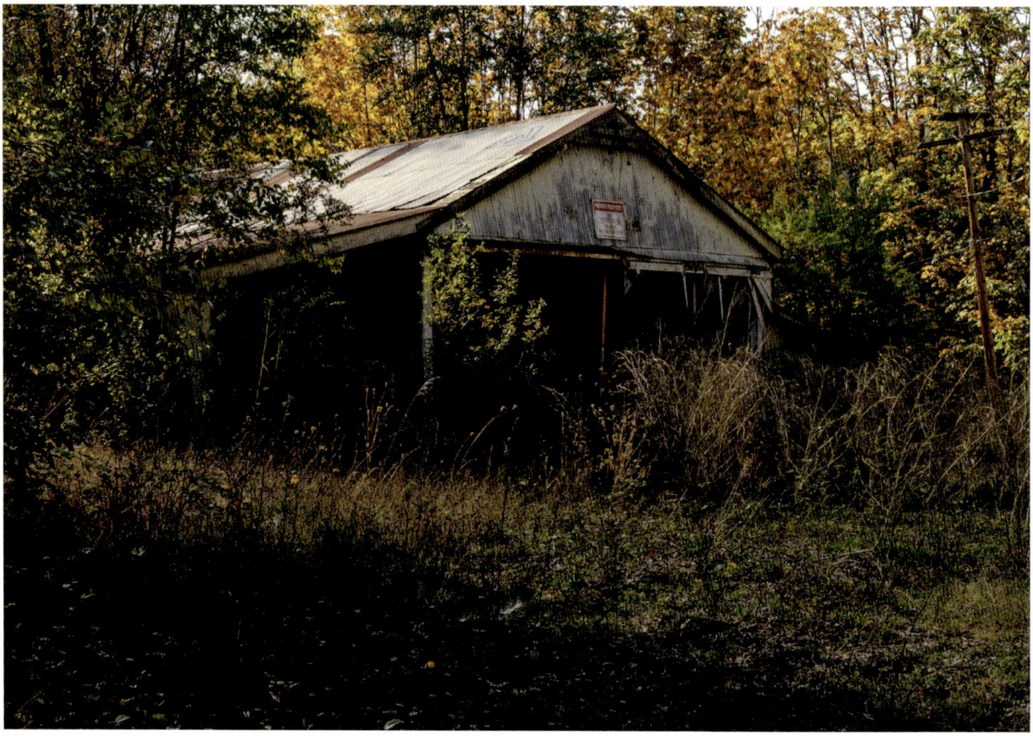

Storage facility that sits on the entrance edge of the property revealing that it is rusted over bare bones.

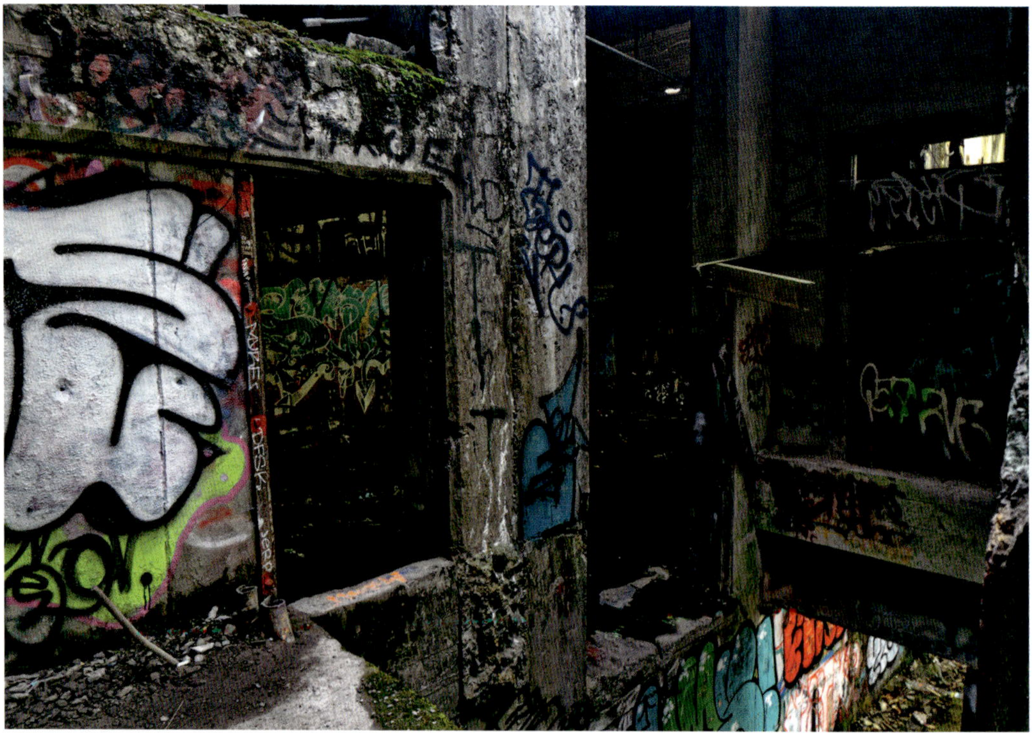

Different levels show areas where floors would connect to other areas, no longer available.

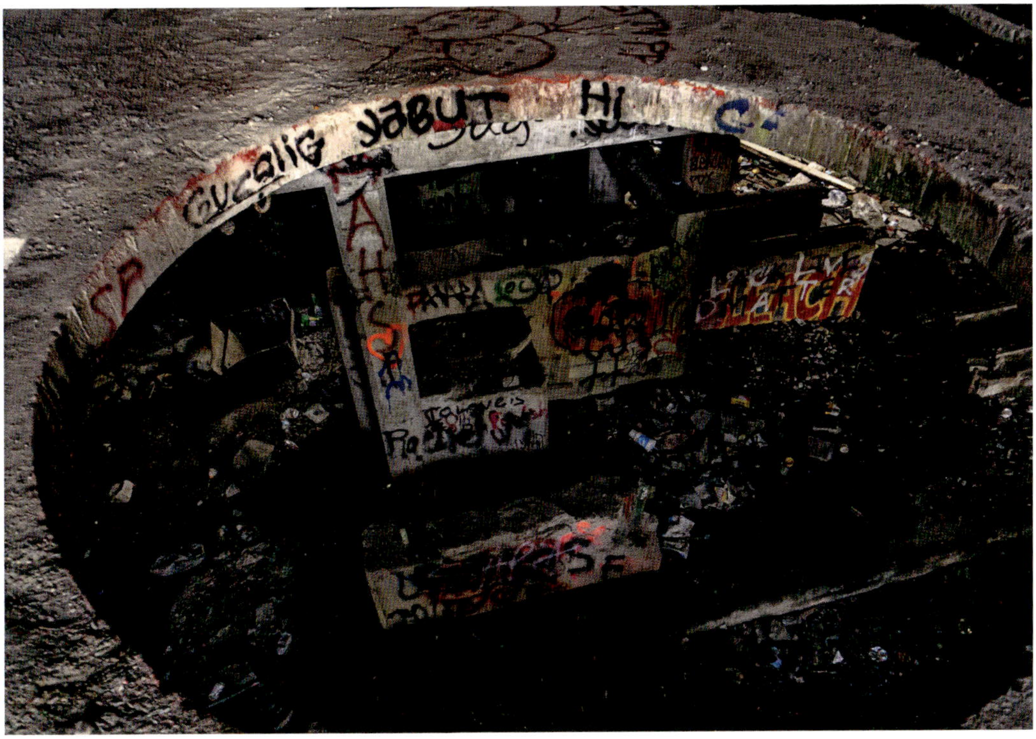

The machinery that once sat here must have been the brains that ran the show.

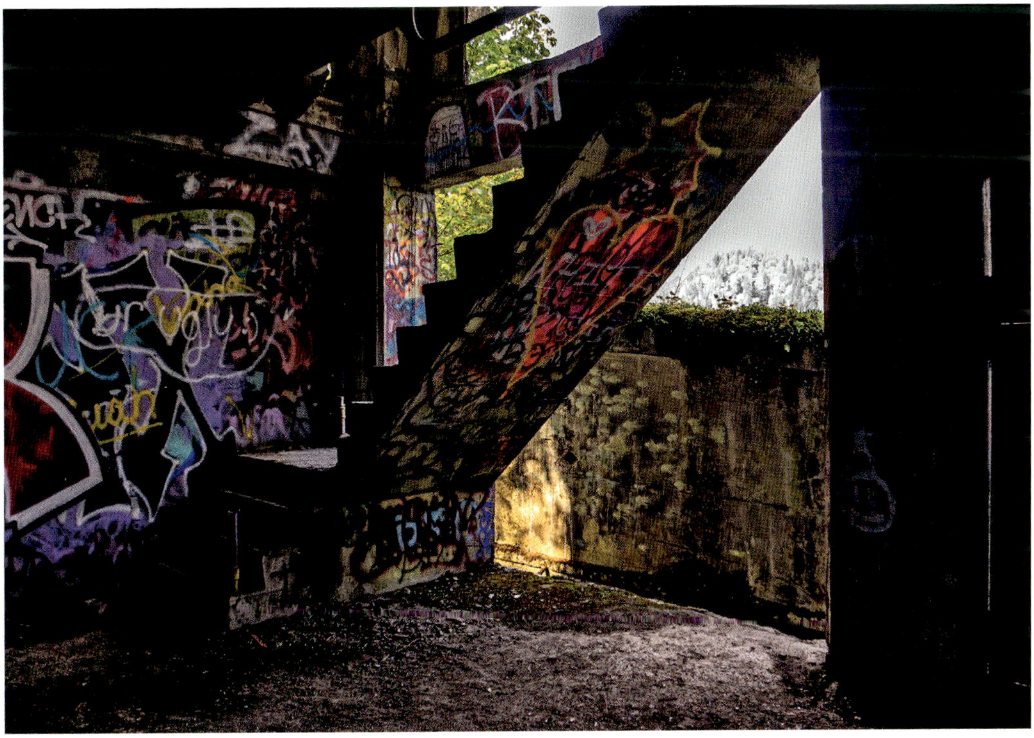

Stairwells offered great views, but also unsafe conditions and should highly be avoided.

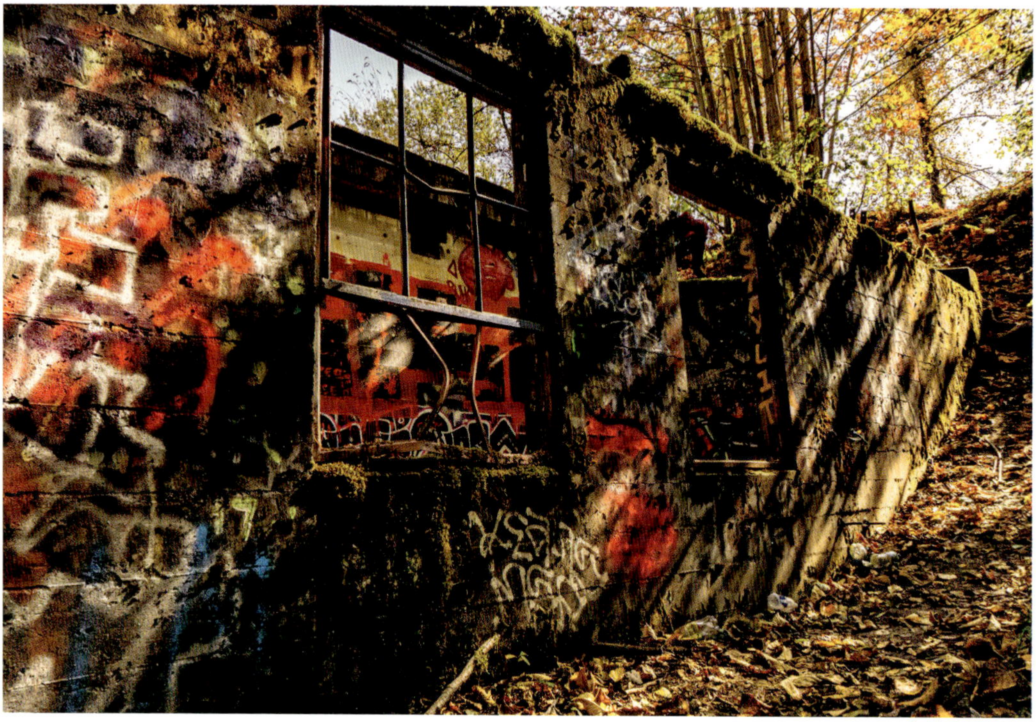

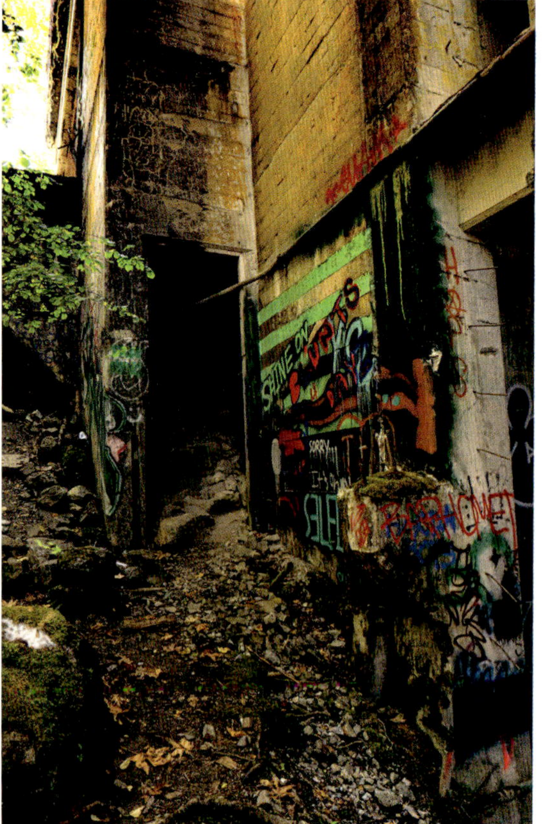


*Above:* Windowsills missing windows line the property line, as sawmills and workshops.

*Left:* An old storage building sits on a different end of the property, hidden from site.

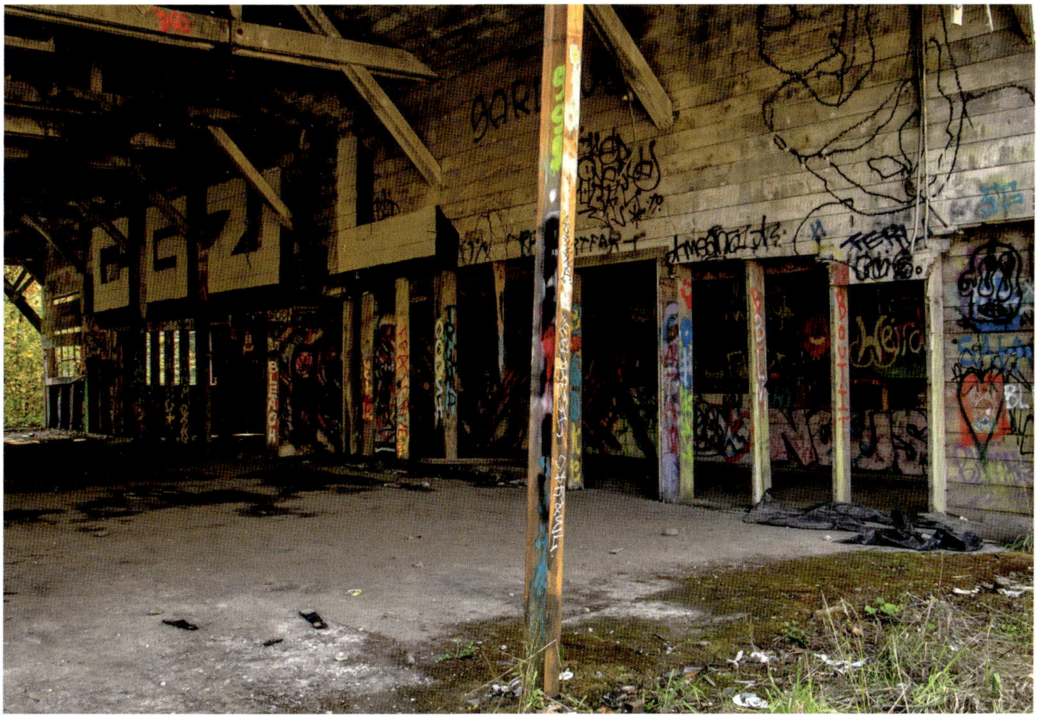

The facility was used for shipping and storage of supplies

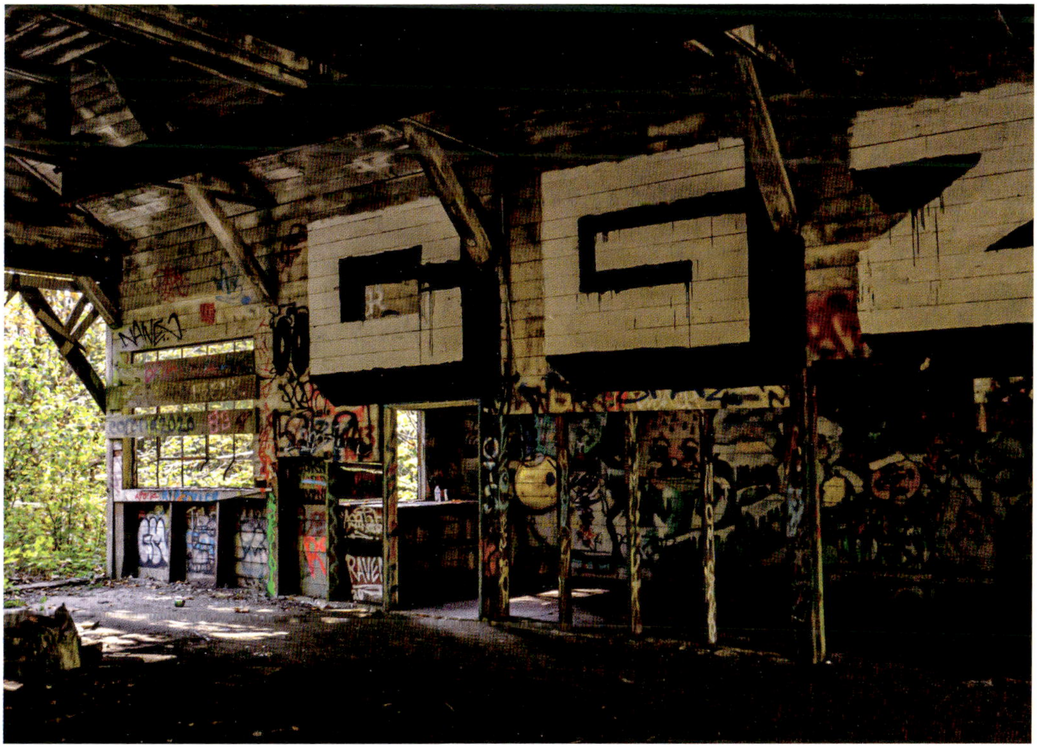

Backside of the storage facility, with an assortment of graffiti from the past fifty years.

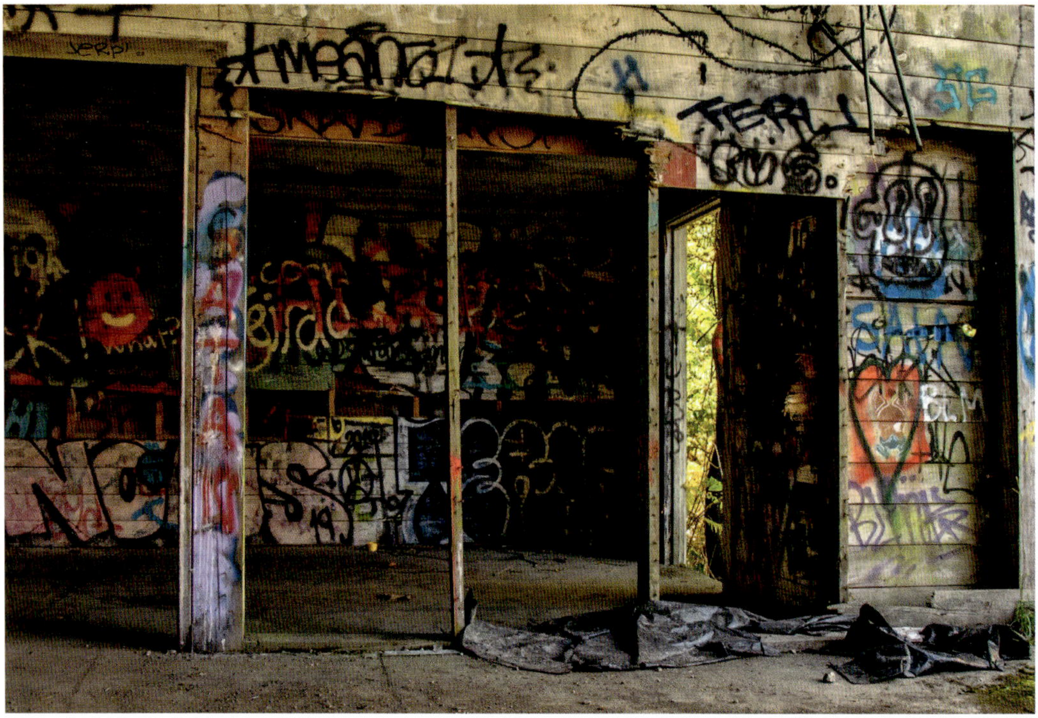

Old office front to the storage and shipping building.

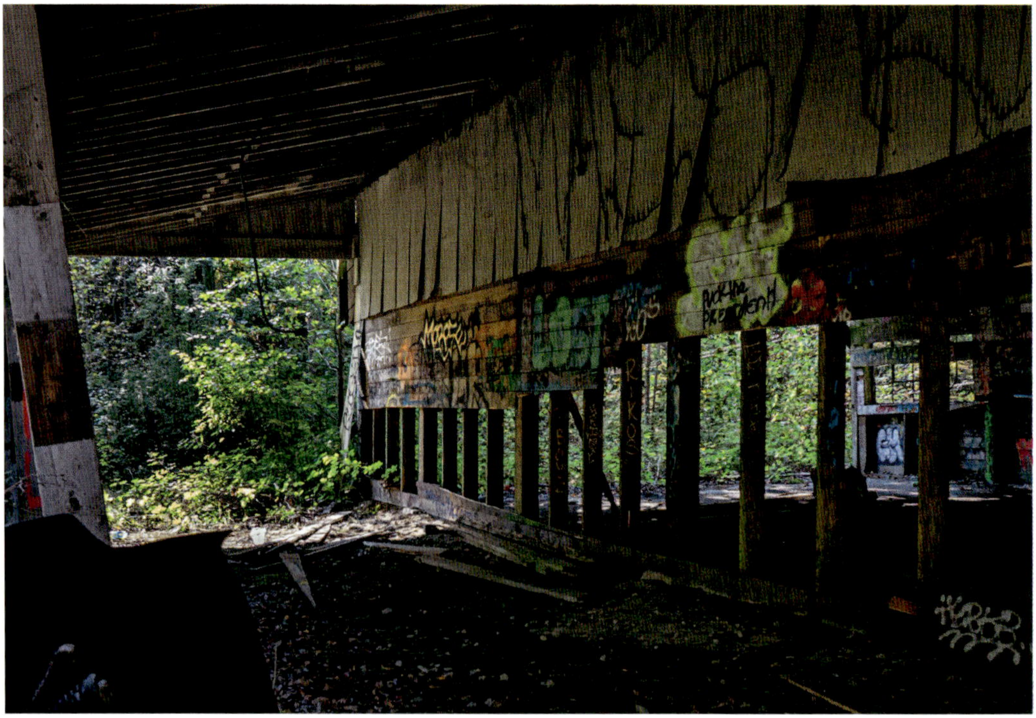

The property also originally had a track that would transport materials from the main building, but shortly after ceased operations.

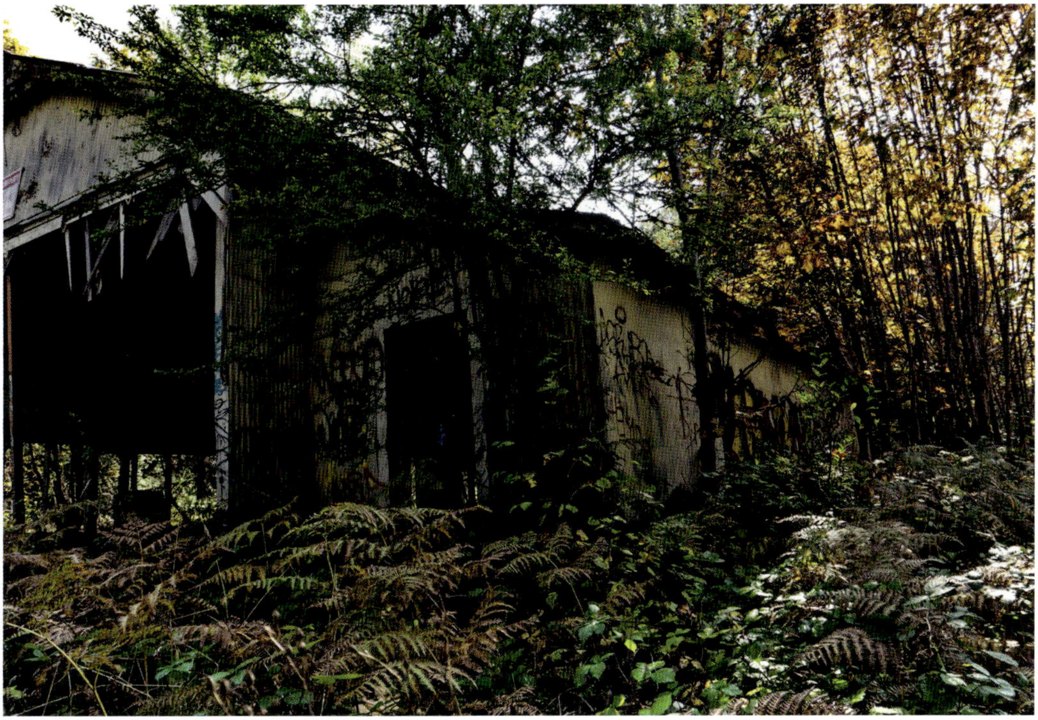

This building upon entering the property would be the first one you would see.

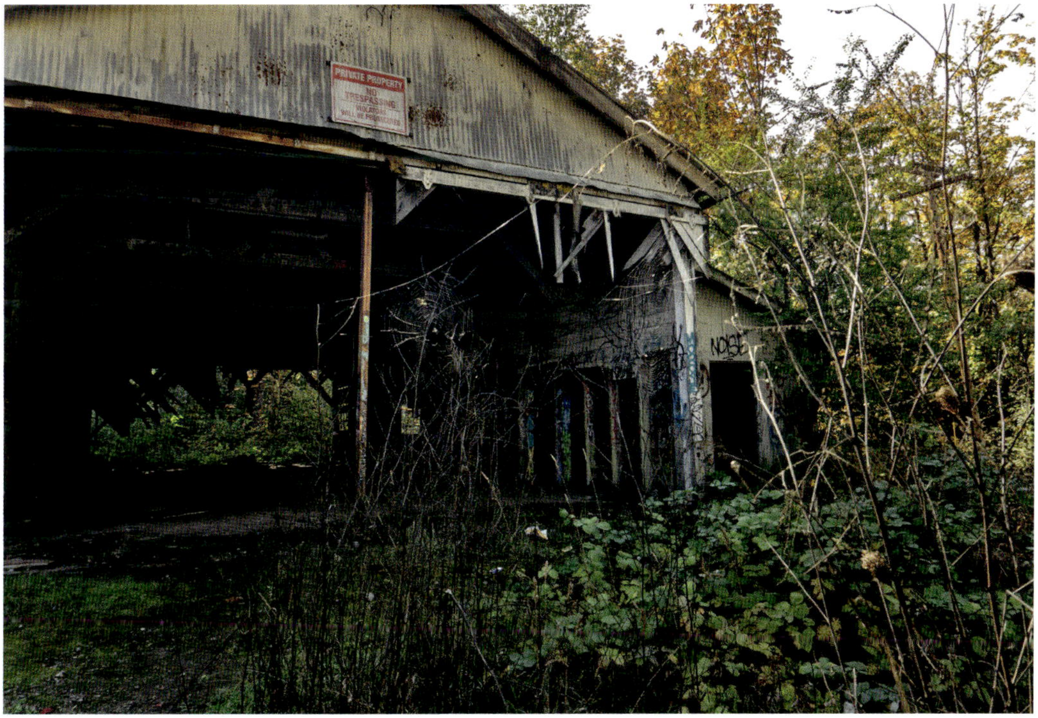

Spiders and cobwebs claim walkways as you approach the building.

# 3

# FARM LIFE

At Northern Hospital's height, the self-sustaining 700-acre horse and dairy farm was the largest of its kind west of the Mississippi. Patients would work on the farm as a form of therapy and made it possible for food to be available for the hospital by providing crops and the daily work that came from the farm. The facility had a full livestock farm of cows, chickens, horses, and more. There was a remarkable number of production facilities like canning, the lumber mill, or the laundry to fill one's day with work. The property offered a wonderful sense of community with a great dose of nature that eventually made it possible to provide food to other hospitals situated in Washington.

On a clear day, one would be able to see Mount Baker in the far background of the campus. Patients were encouraged to socialize at events, and they even dyed their own eggs from the farm on Easter and hid them throughout the property for others to join in on Easter egg hunts. On some of the barns, you can see copper ventilations on the roofs that were even handmade by some of the patients. The colony provided therapeutic routines for those mentally capable to participate, which not all patients could.

By the amount of medical breakthrough drugs produced in the 1950s, it allowed the mentally challenged to work on themselves in order to become independent members of society. It became more socially acceptable to no longer confine these people but, better yet, reintroduce them back into society. They were able to get through a day's chores without mental disturbances, as well as make their own decisions on how to live or if they needed treatment. While Northern Hospital was still operating some of the functioning patients able to control themselves and cope with their internal issues, were even able to travel to Bug and shop without hospital

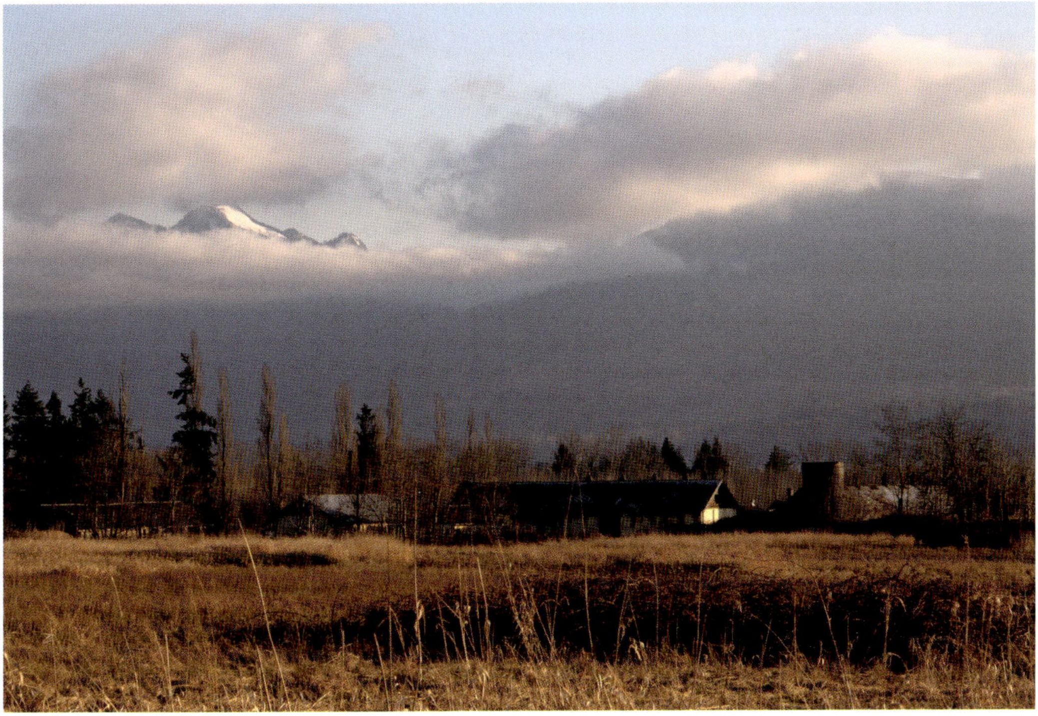

Northern Hospital's farm offered beautiful magical views of Mount Baker.

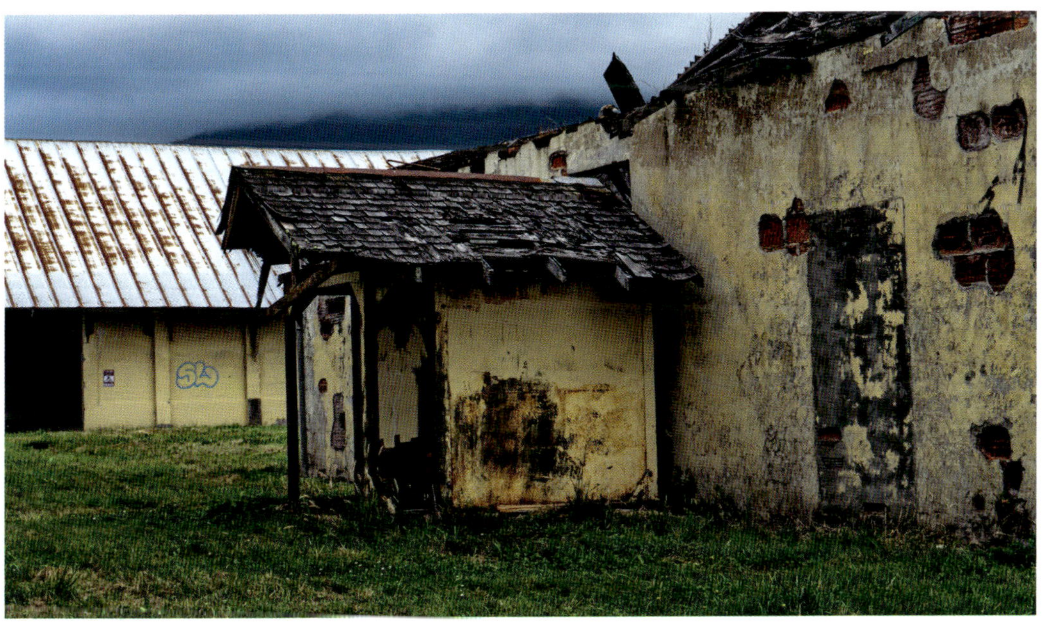

Concrete and paint aged on buildings with shingles barely hanging on.

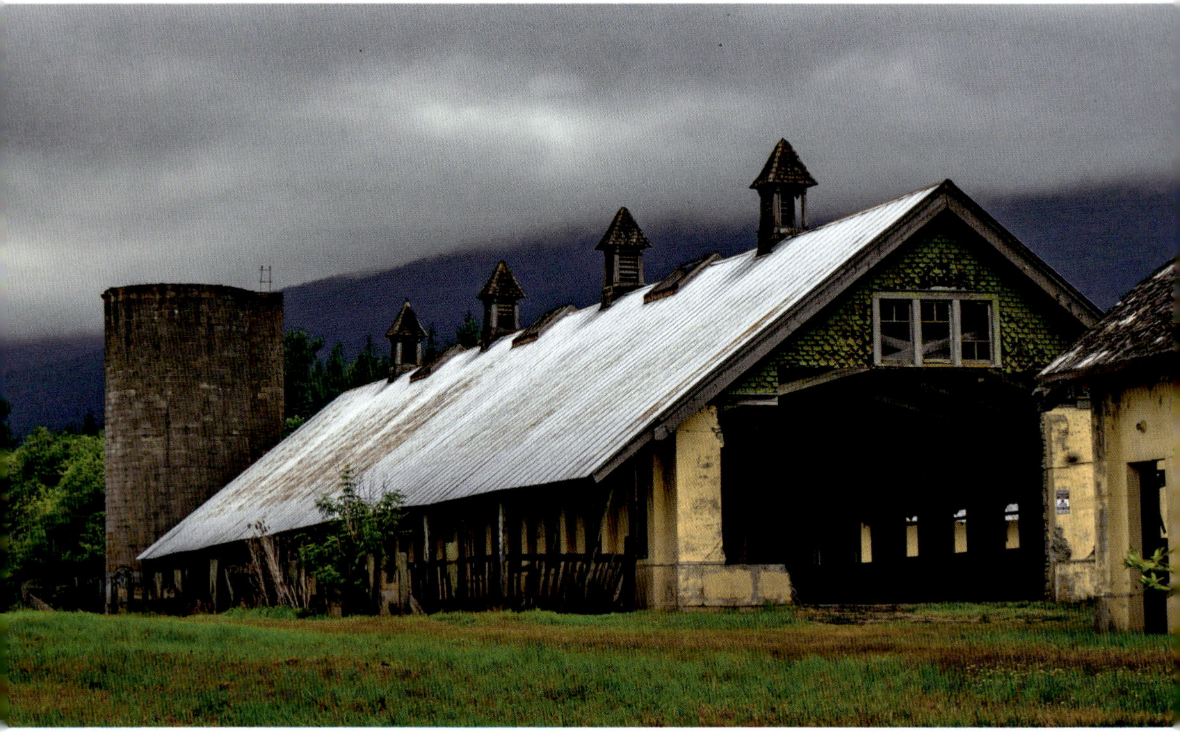

Horse barn with green-painted shingles and silo in backdrop.

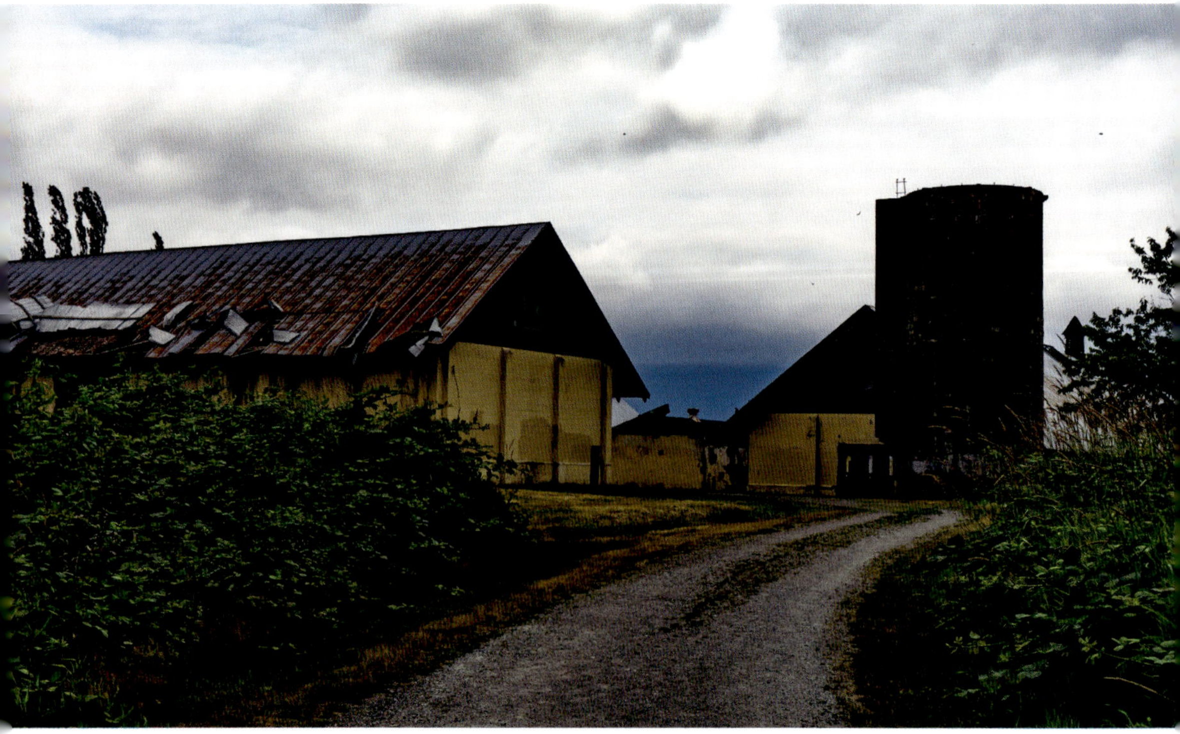

Old back driveway into the Northern Hospital farm, no longer active.

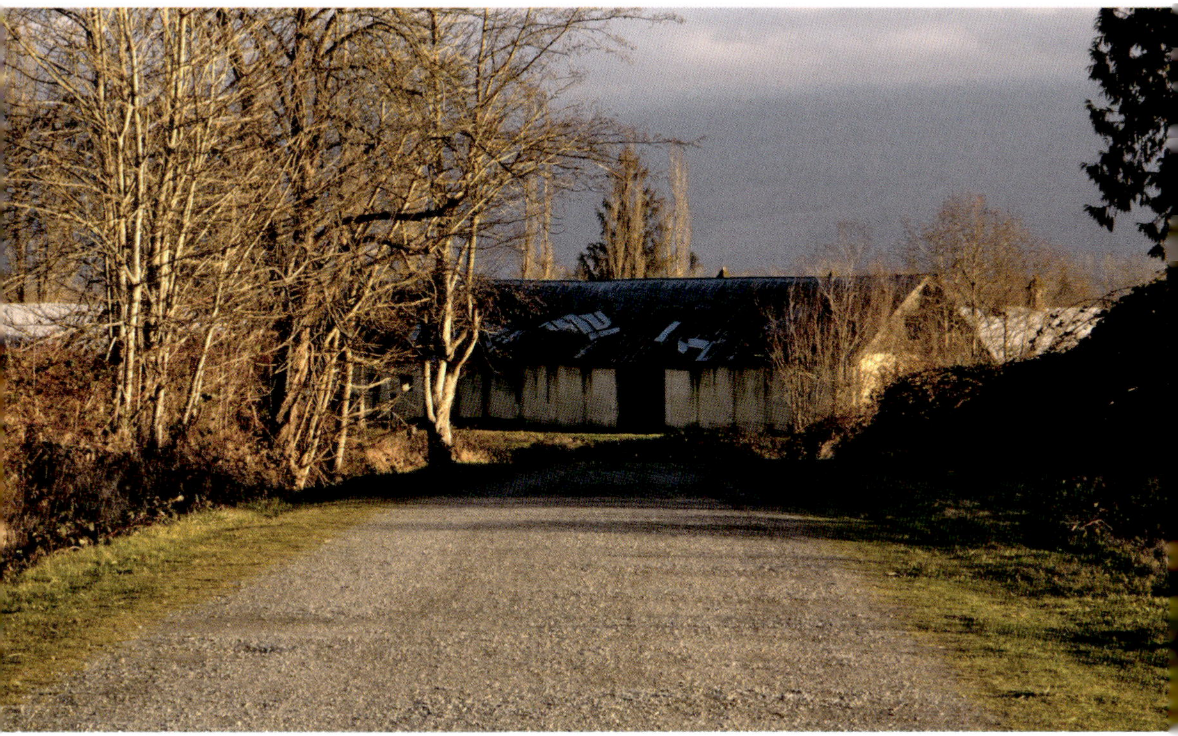

Calf and grain barn, one of the largest barn's on the farm.

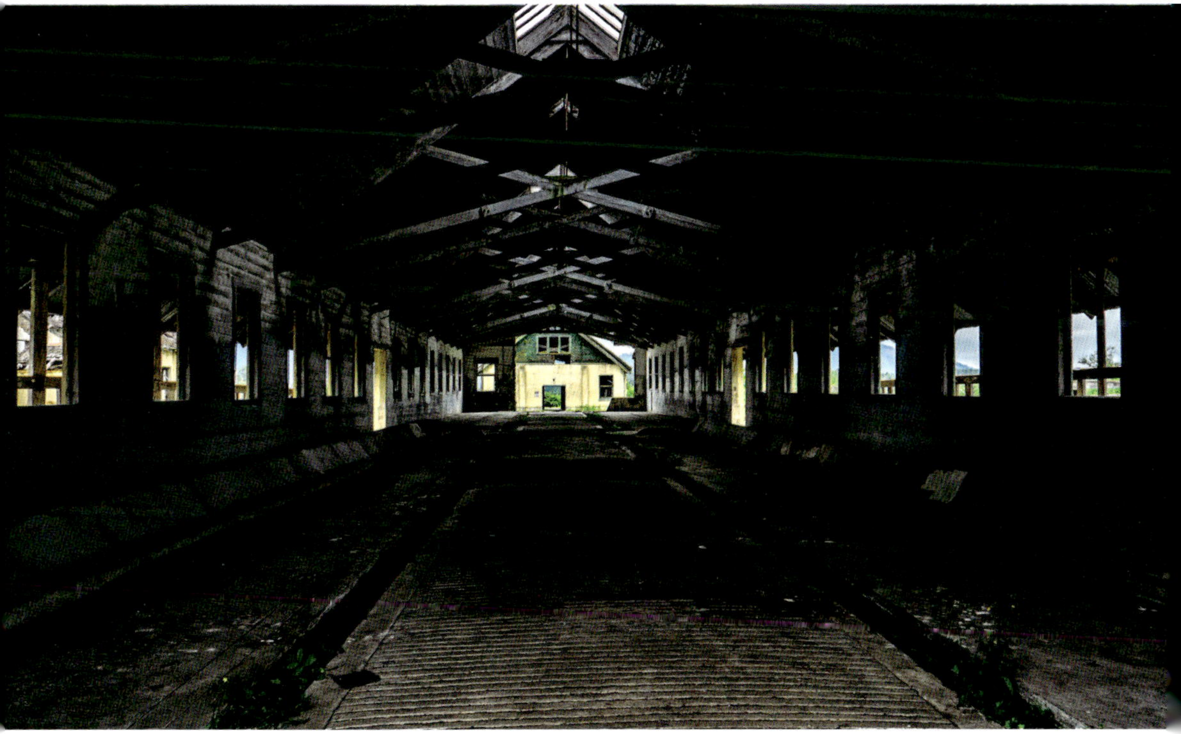

This barn did not offer much to the imagination, no stalls, no separate aisles, just wide open space, ceilings, and windows.

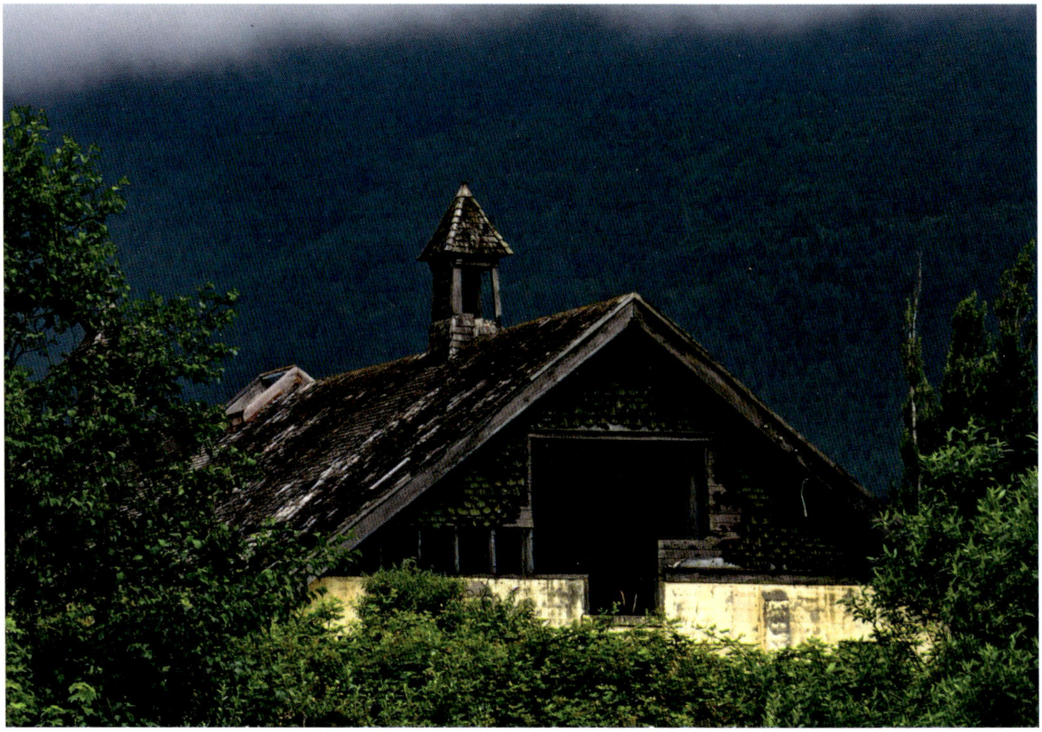

The metal ventilation structures on the barns were built by the patients of Northern Hospital.

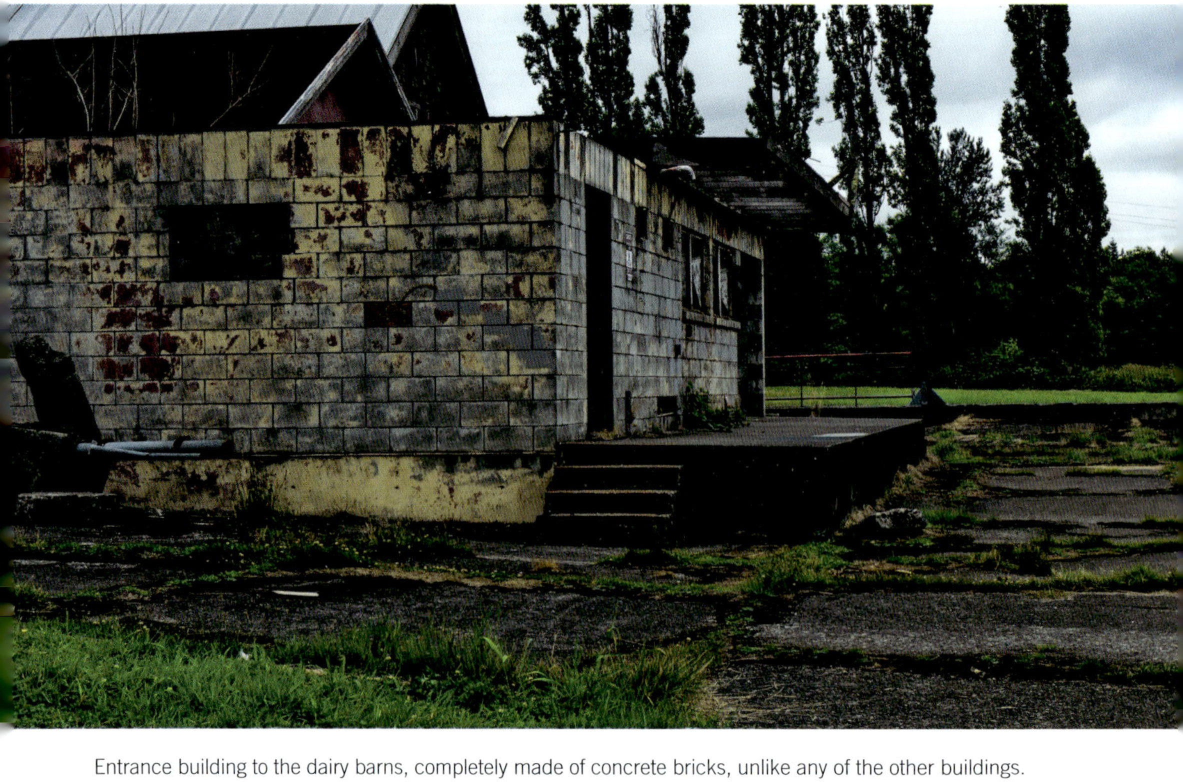

Entrance building to the dairy barns, completely made of concrete bricks, unlike any of the other buildings.

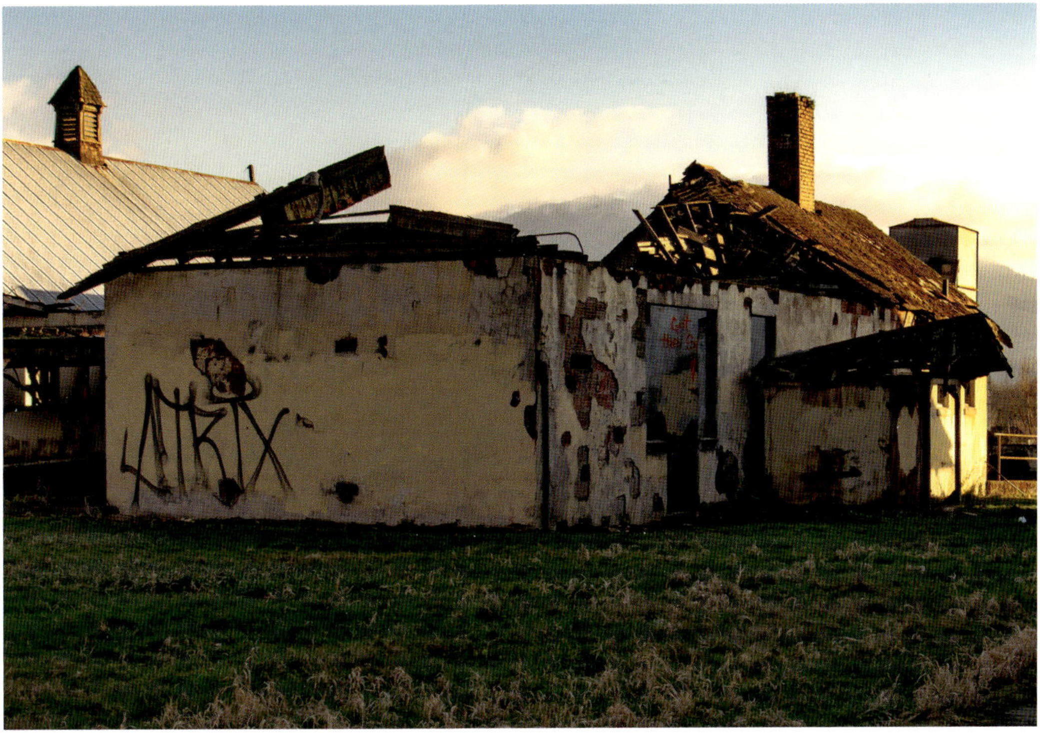

The roof collided into itself on one of the dairy barn buildings.

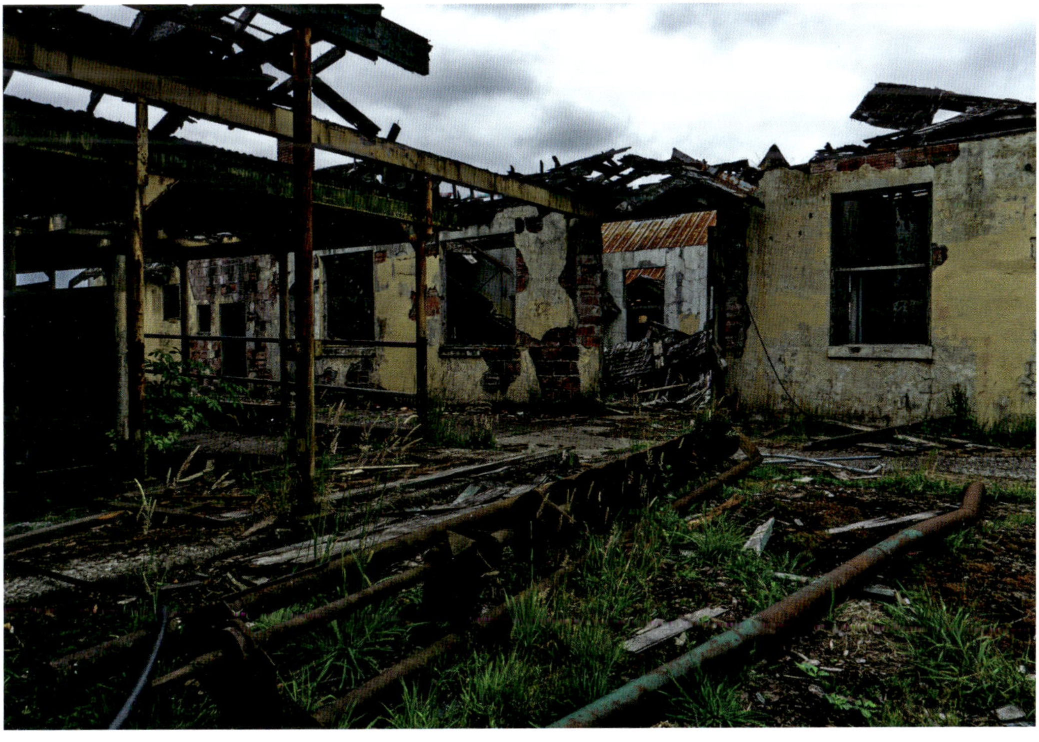

Old farm equipment found between buildings.

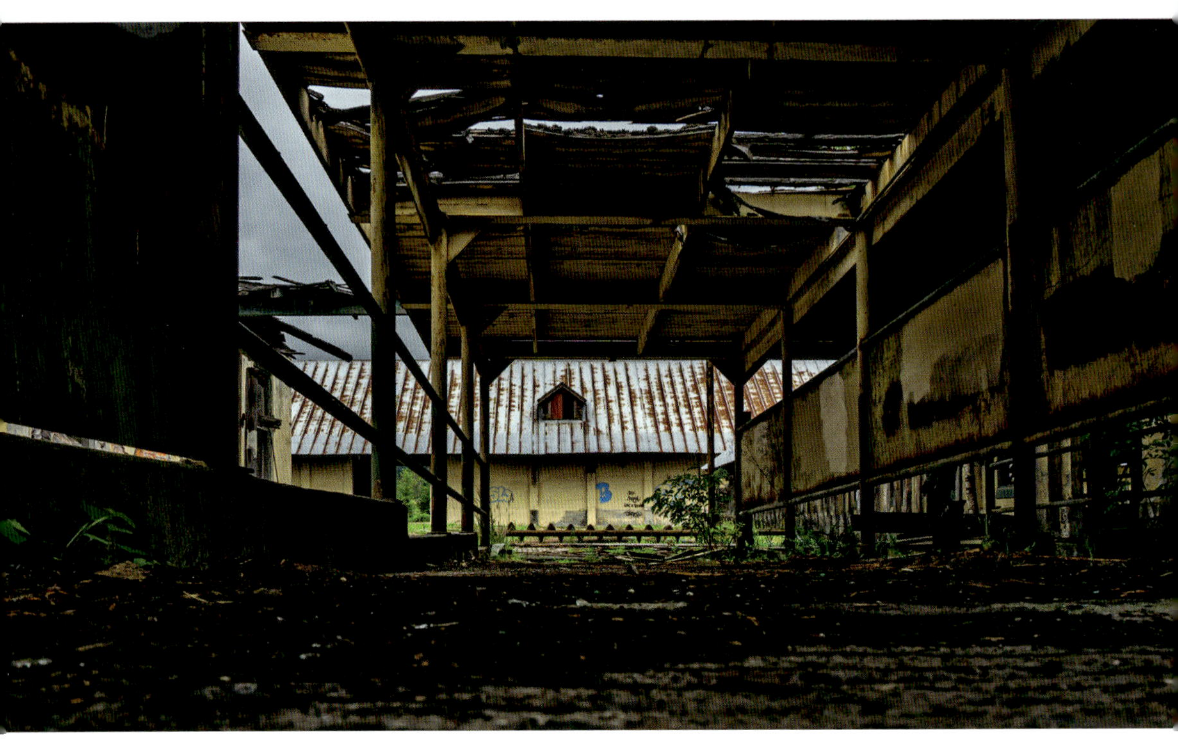

Dairy barn entrance for its cows, with most of its roof still intact.

personnel supervision as part of their treatment regime. The times were changing before our eyes.

Located in the far-back corner of the property behind the facilities gymnasium, there is a cemetery with a majority of unmarked graves. There are approximately 1,500 graves and only one tombstone. Only a handful of the graves have markers, and of these, they bear only initials and a number. As years progressed, new drugs made mental institutions more and more obsolete.

It was at this time that standard medical procedures and drugs began to get questioned by doctors. People started to demand to know what was going on behind closed doors. Were the staff treating the patients carelessly or harsh? Additionally, sociologists argued that institutions like this would create a dependency and cause people to believe they needed to be institutionalized. It became a time of great unknowing for mental hospitals but positive progressive changes were coming for the better.

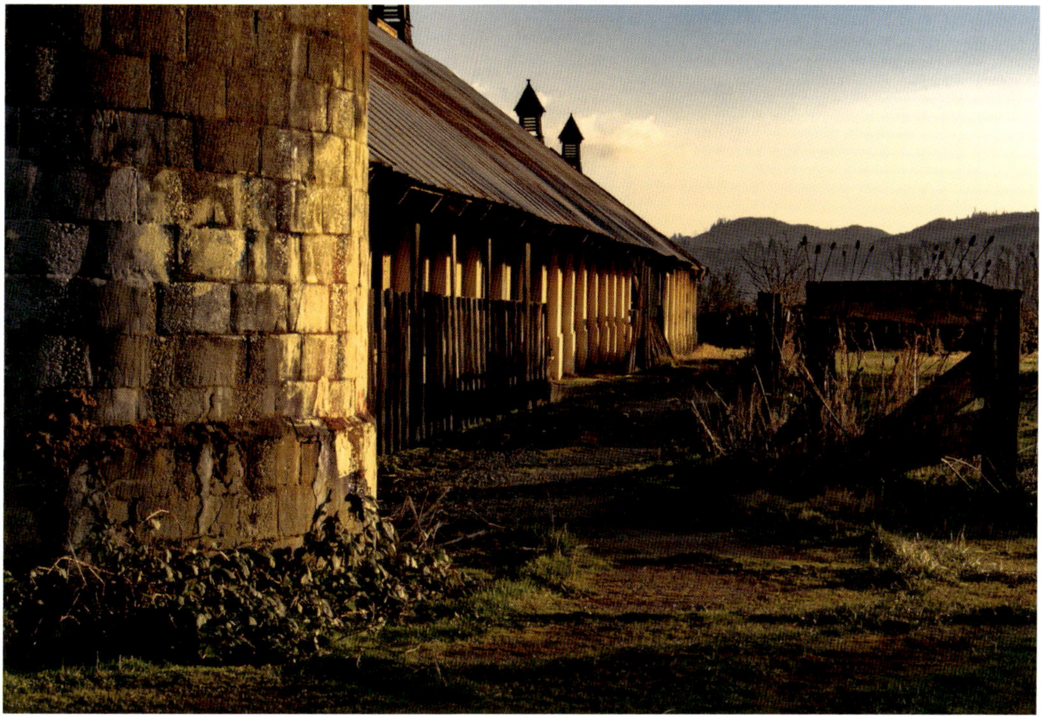

Beautiful sunset along the Cascade Range, with the horse barn and silo on display.

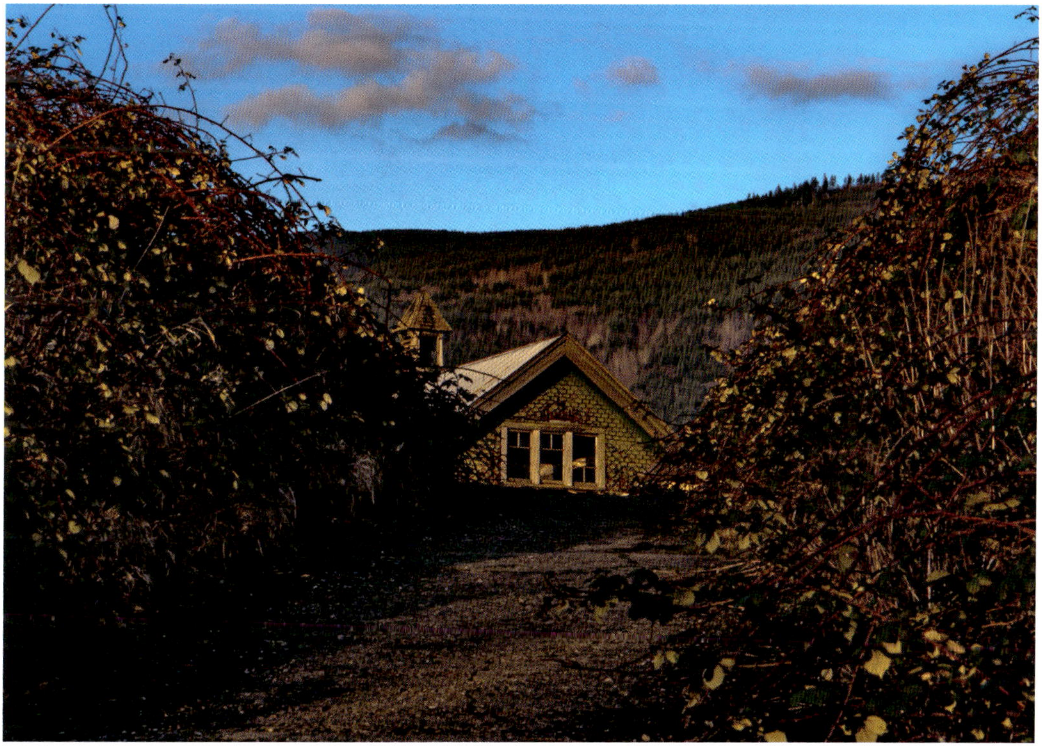

Walking among vines and barn roofs; this will be the first peak you will see upon entering.

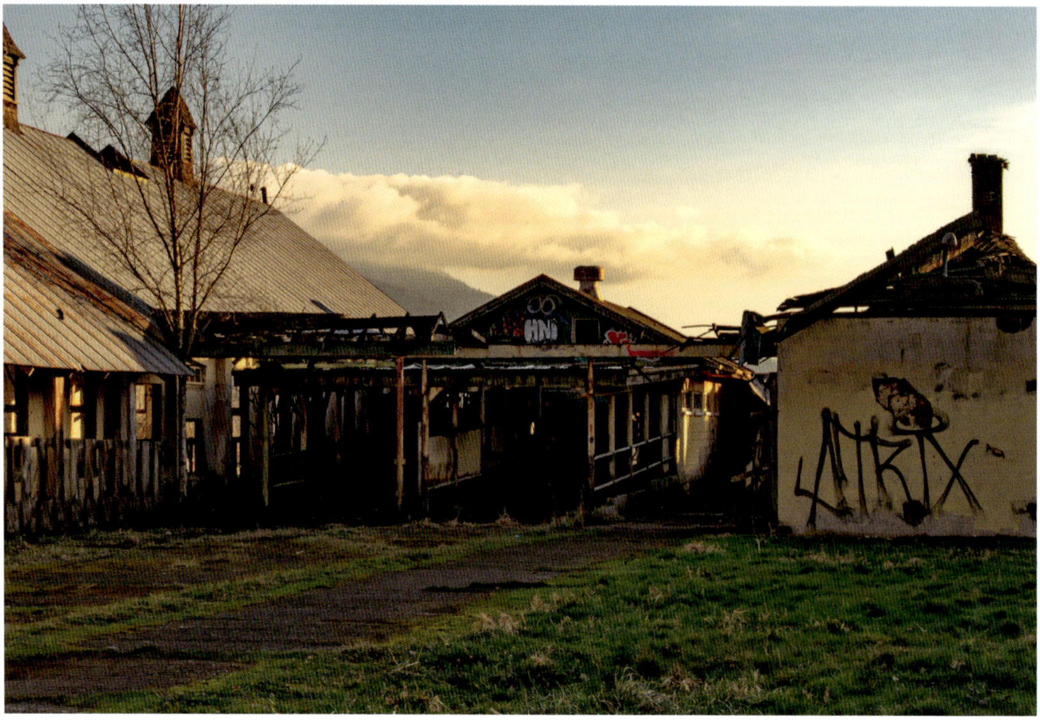

The property is well maintained, so even though buildings have collapsed on themselves, it is still safe enough to appreciate from a distance.

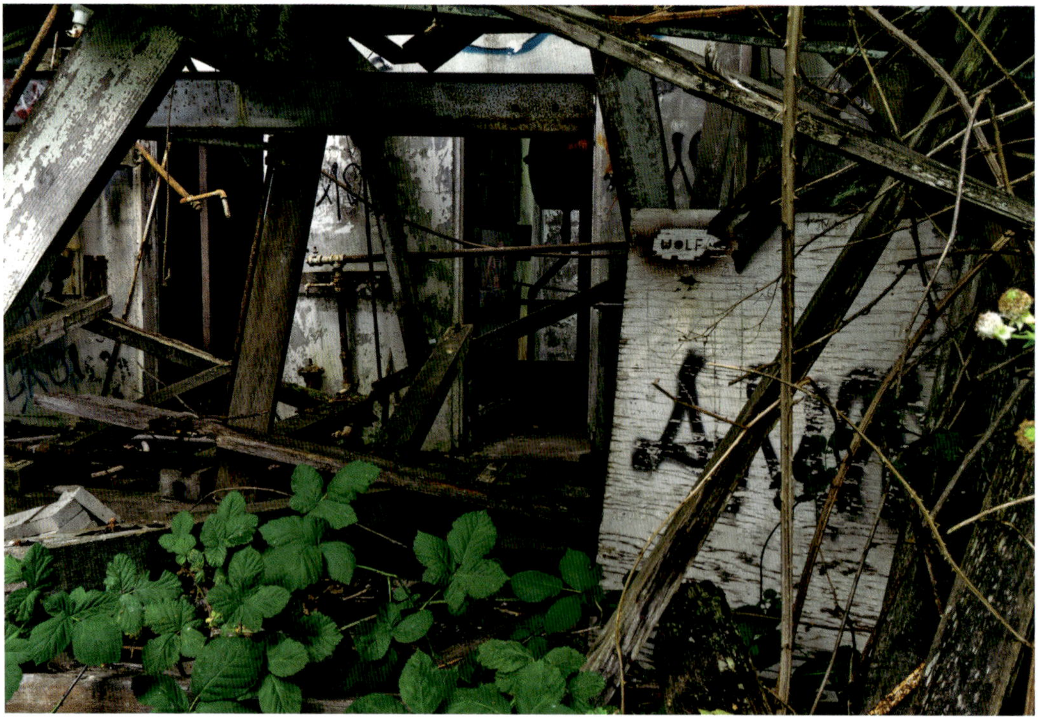

Lockers still somehow remain in staff quarters with some areas of roofing entirely missing.

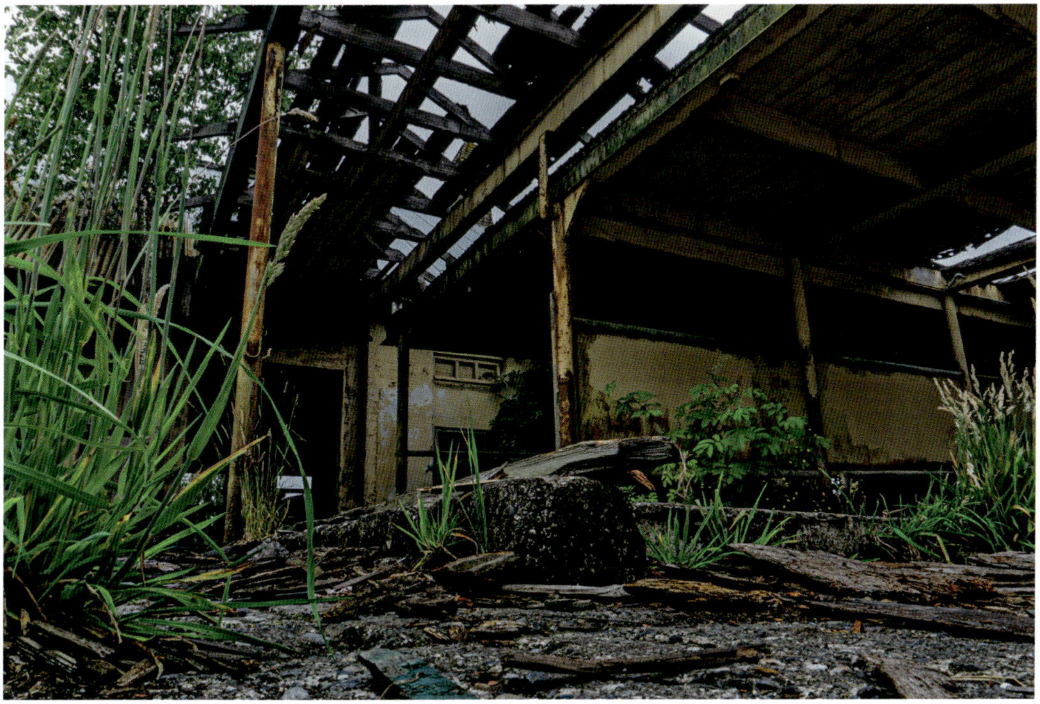

There is more to the eye of the stories and lives of the untold.

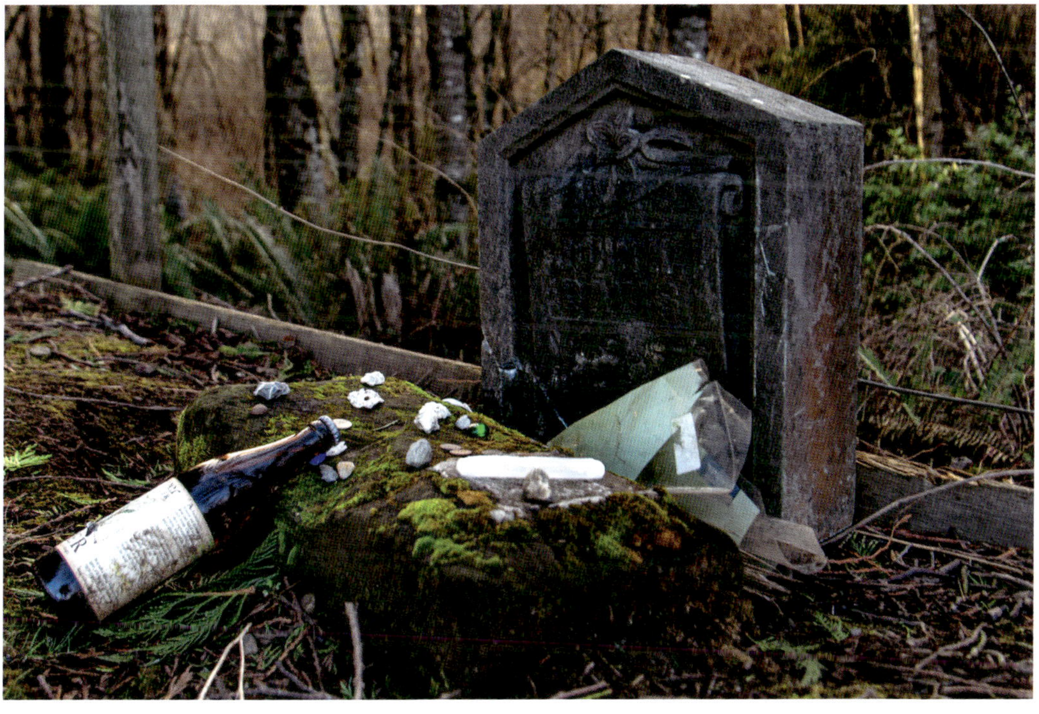

The 1.5-acre cemetery, located on the far eastern side of the grounds, has 1,487 gravesites and one gravestone. Most gravesites are unmarked and swampy—your shoes will be swallowed whole for those trying to pay respects to those unknown sites.

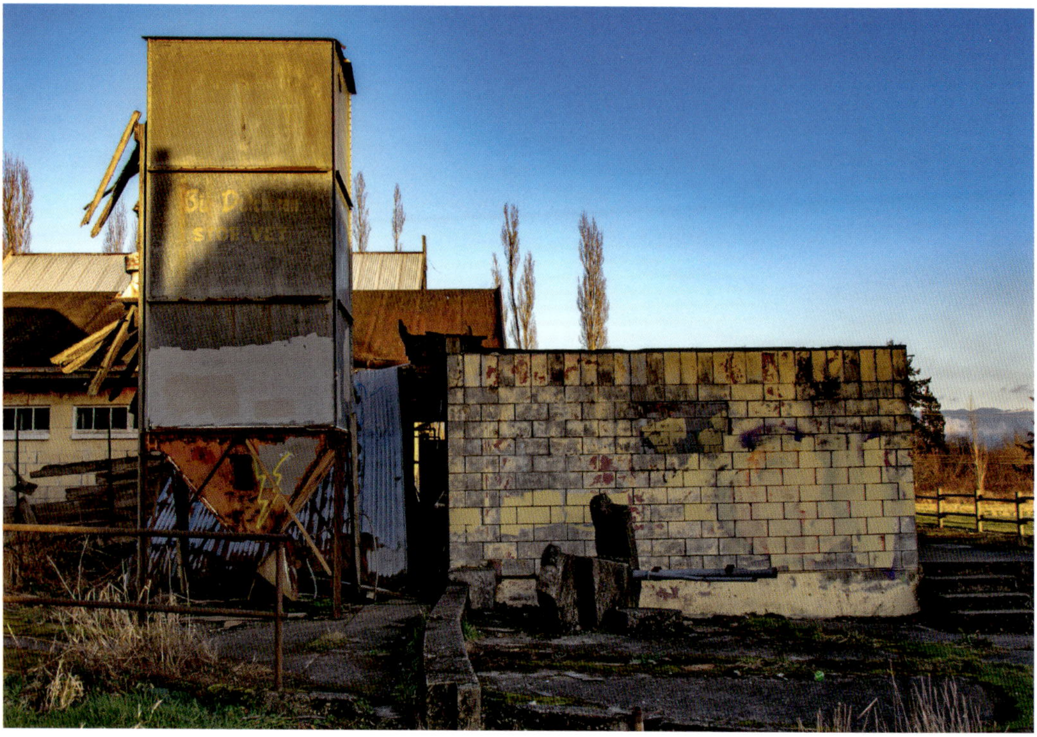

Only beams remain in buildings further out from the trails.

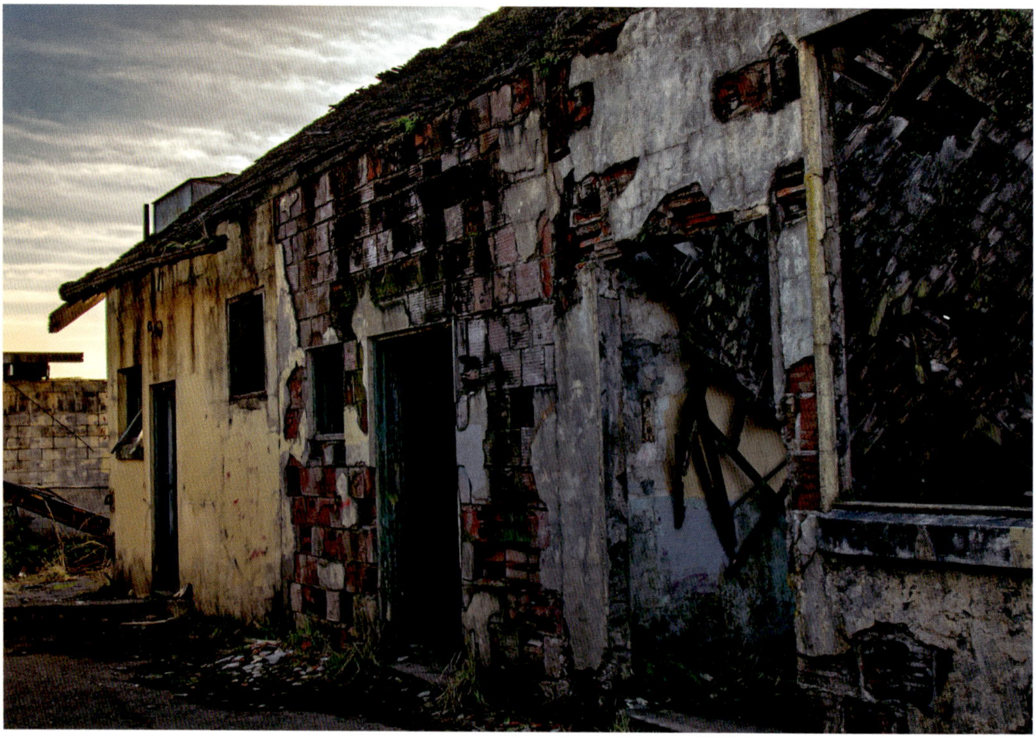

Many obstructions and machinery line the floor of this facility.

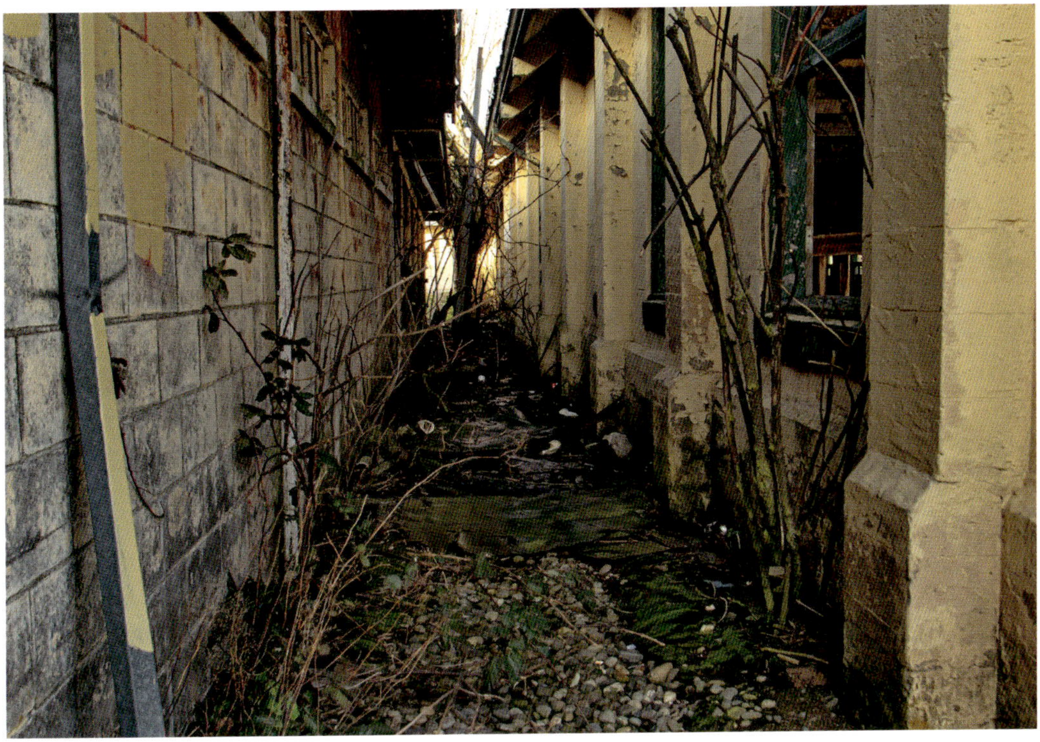

There is a common theme of moss everywhere, as these buildings were not built for wet climates.

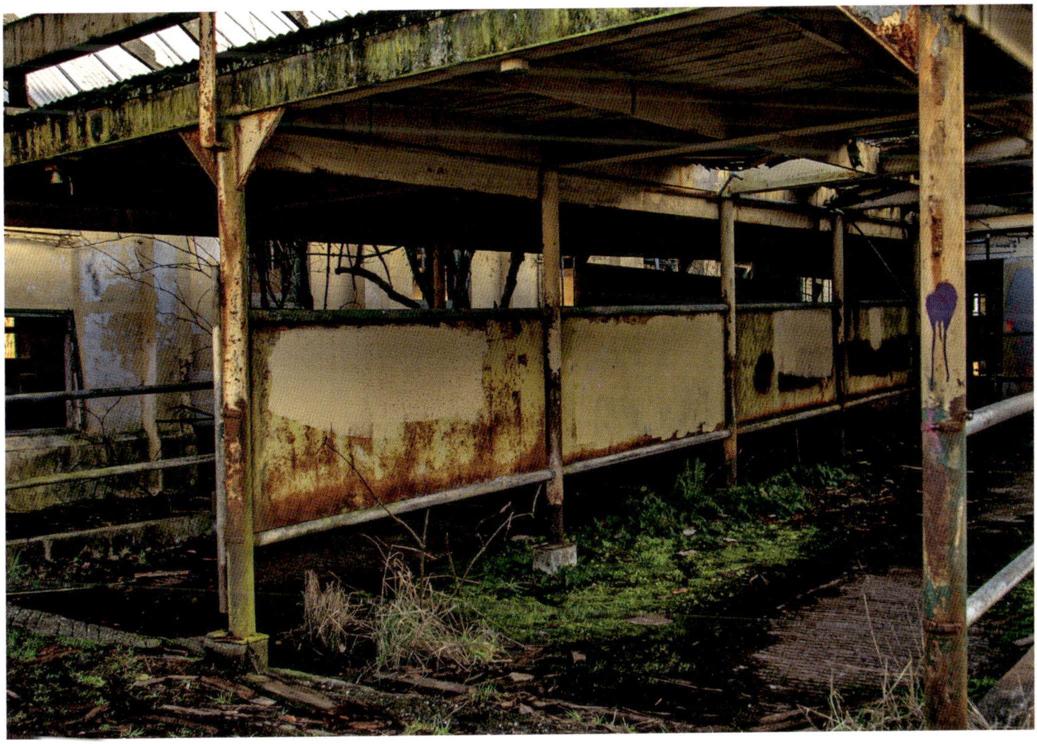

Some buildings are even hard to approach, with nature claiming it.

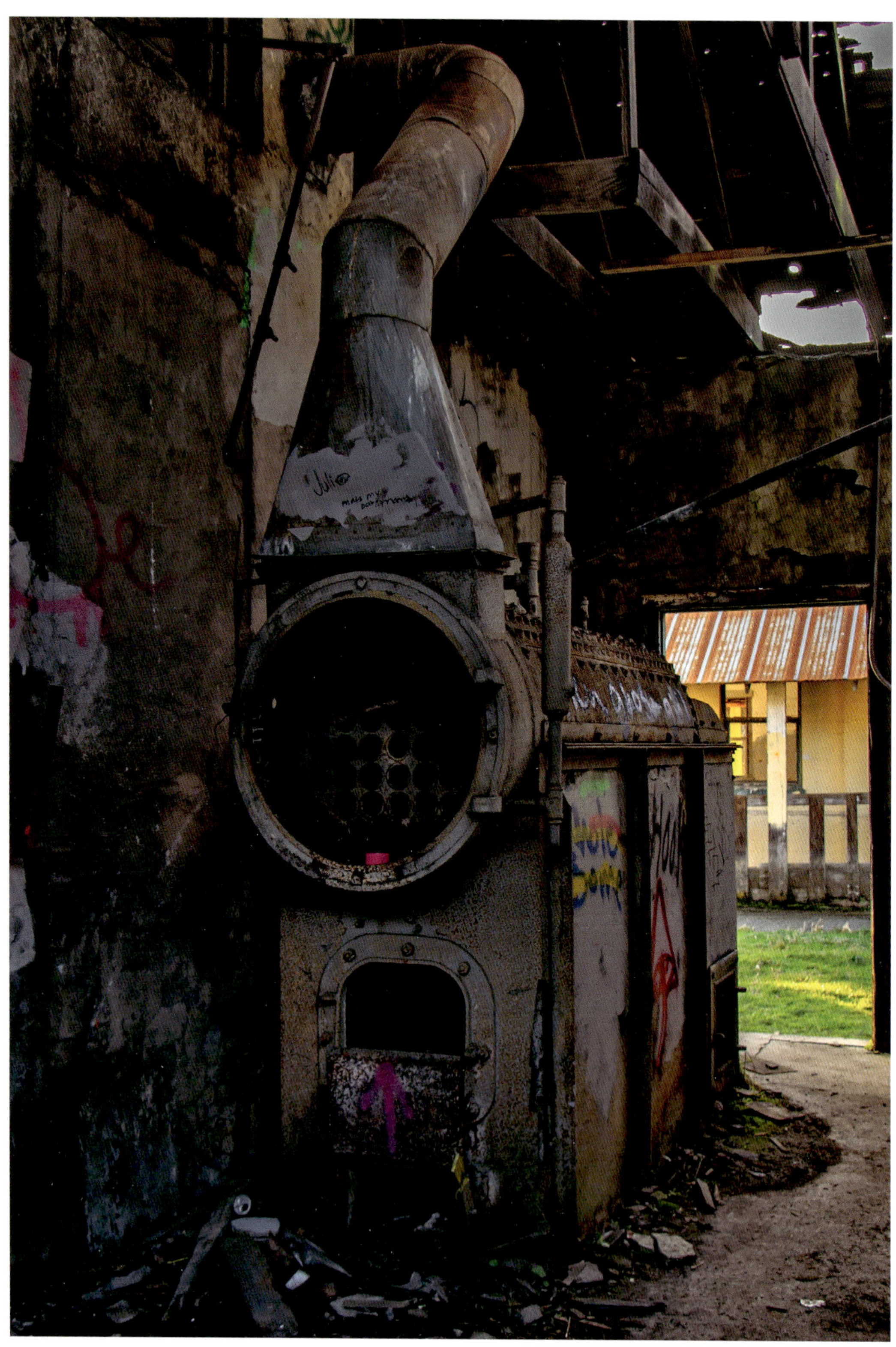

Graffiti from many passers-by.

# 4

# DEATH

As the 1960s approached, so did the powerful movements of health, science, and environmental protection. North Hospital was approaching its final years as more drugs became reliable for patients who no longer needed treatment. In 1964, the Wilderness Act passed, allowing some federal land to be deemed wilderness that prohibited all types of development aside from recreational hiking trails. In 1968, environmentalists successfully influenced the creation of North Cascades National Park's 1.3 million-acre complex with an additional 685,000-acre wilderness area. This would now protect the area to help preserve the wilderness with only a few roads to gain access to the parks. Additionally, this prevented any more industrial organizations from exploiting the lands, preventing future pollution occurrence. By 1972, the oldest state road in Washington became the state's longest highway, running 246 miles across Highway 20, also known as North Cascades Highway. This highway would feature a beautiful scenic route of the North Cascades Mountain Range, the most abundant glacial system in the United States. In 1973, the Endangered Species Act passed, requiring the U.S Fish and Wildlife Service to protect all members of the forest's ecosystem. It identified threatened plants and animals and federal agencies were required to protect and promote the recovery of these species.

Eventually, by 1976, the Northern Hospital closed its doors and the patients were ready to re-enter society. This caused a huge downfall in the town's economy, as patients and staff would frequent it. The farm and grounds were donated to Skagit County, which was then turned into a public recreation area where visitors can explore outside the horse and dairy barns. Some of the hospital buildings have been updated and have new purposes, while others are closed off and building doors are sealed shut.

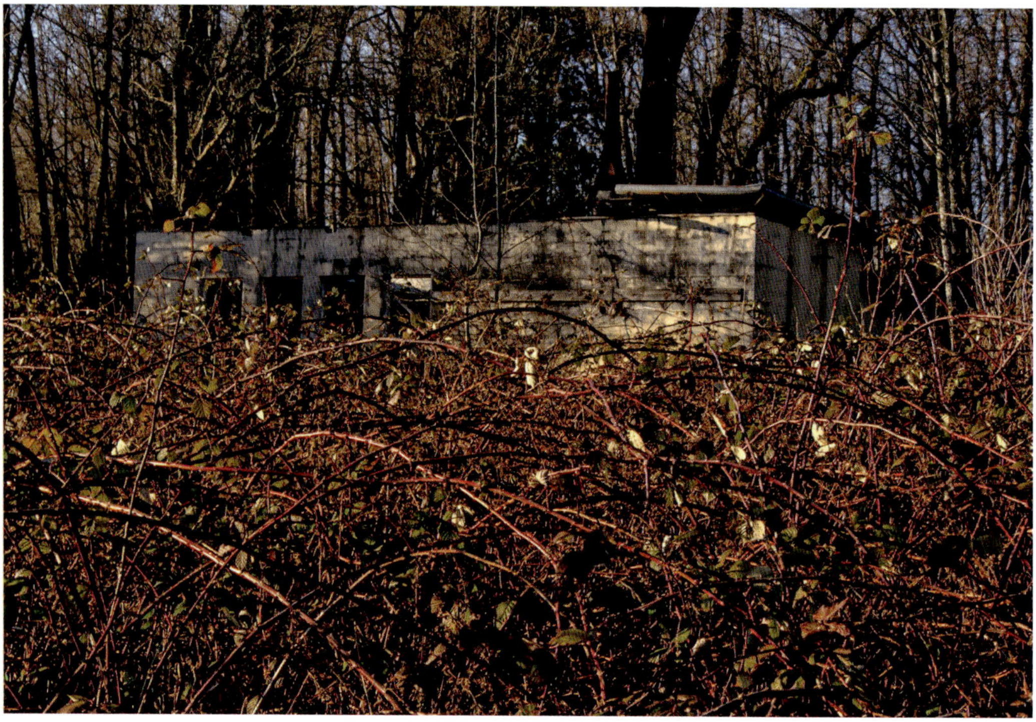

The Northern Hospital's crematorium, hidden from the rest of the campus, was built years after opening when its need for handling patients' remains were demanded.

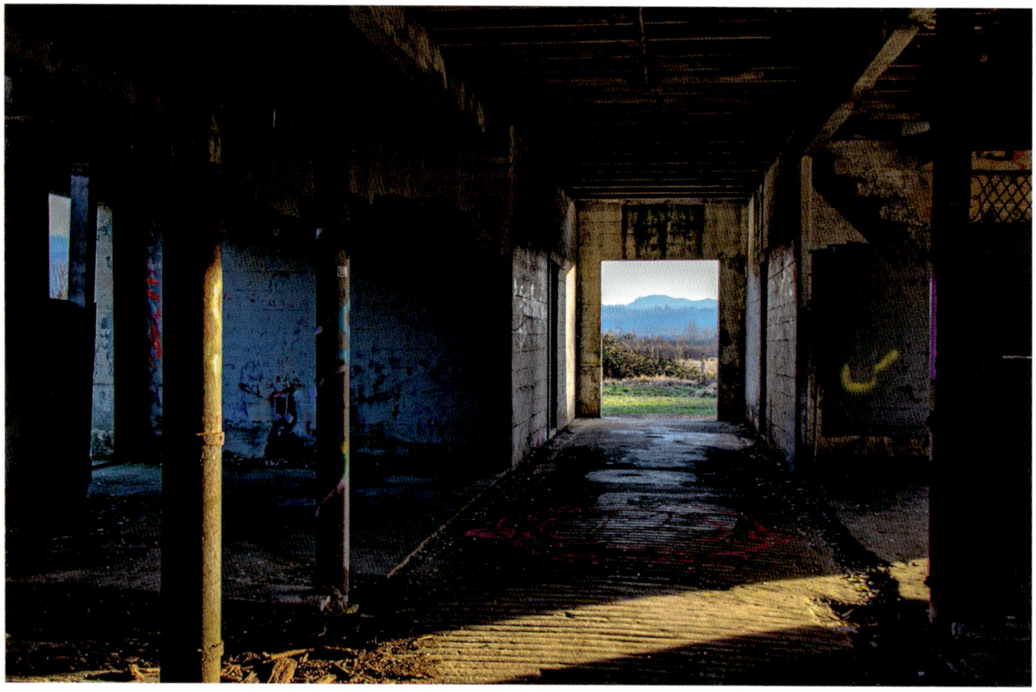

Thorns and moss are a losing battle the closer you approach the buildings. Old machinery rusts over and nails stick out everywhere.

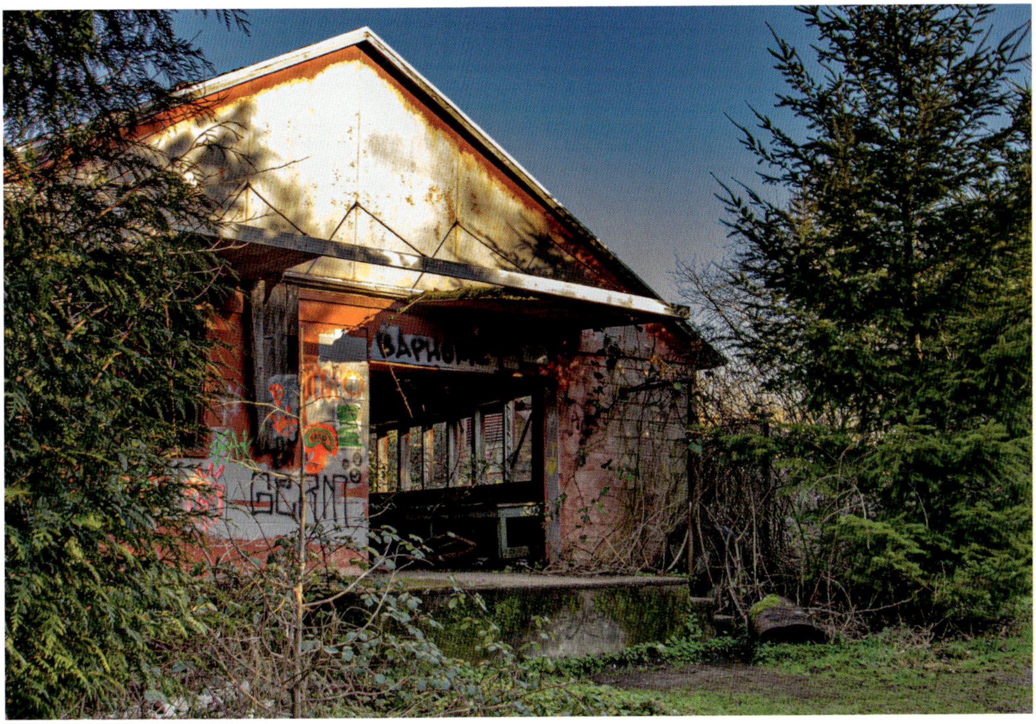

Rotting shingles finally caved in on itself and not much floor was left to this barn.

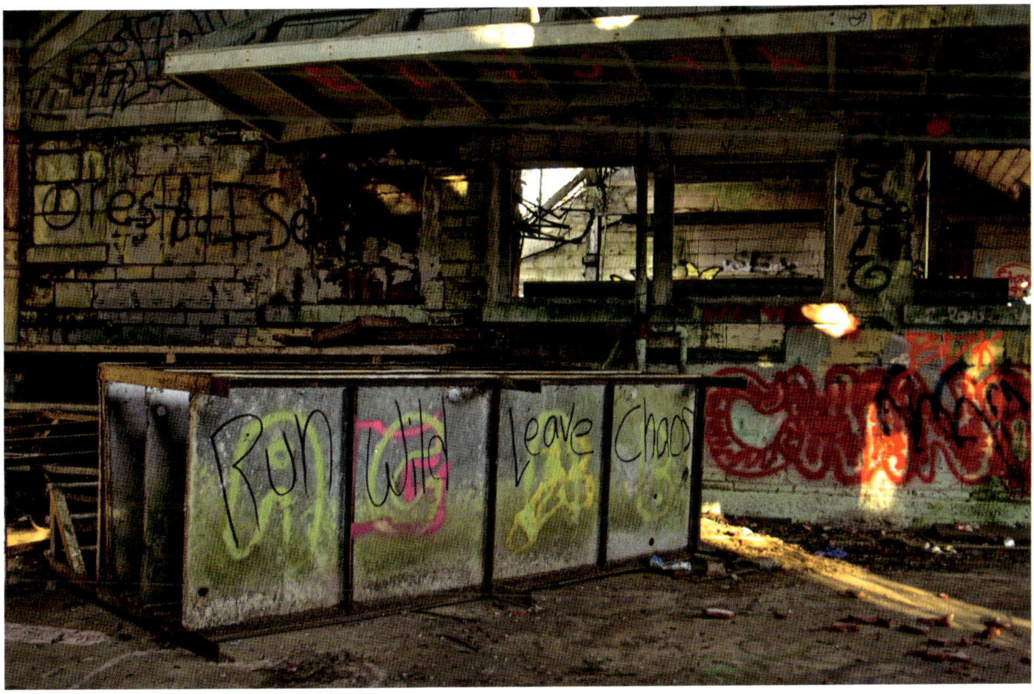

Many of the findings can be seen along doorways along the trails on the property.

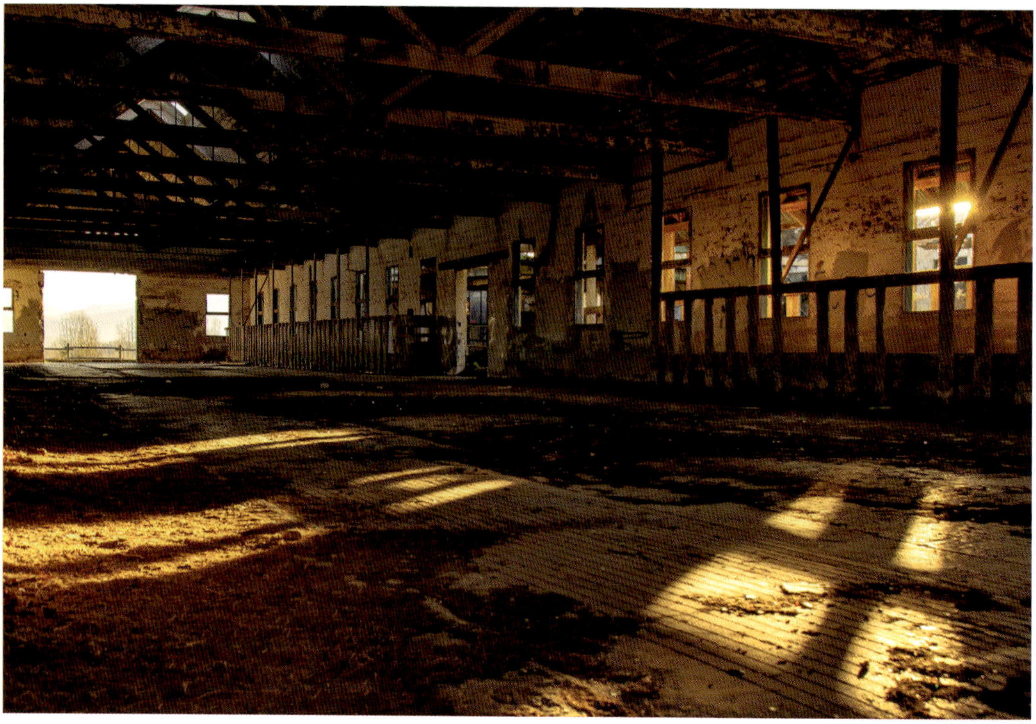

This one particular horse barn was in better condition than other barns on the campus. Wide open space with a high arched ceiling that still had most of its beams surprisingly.

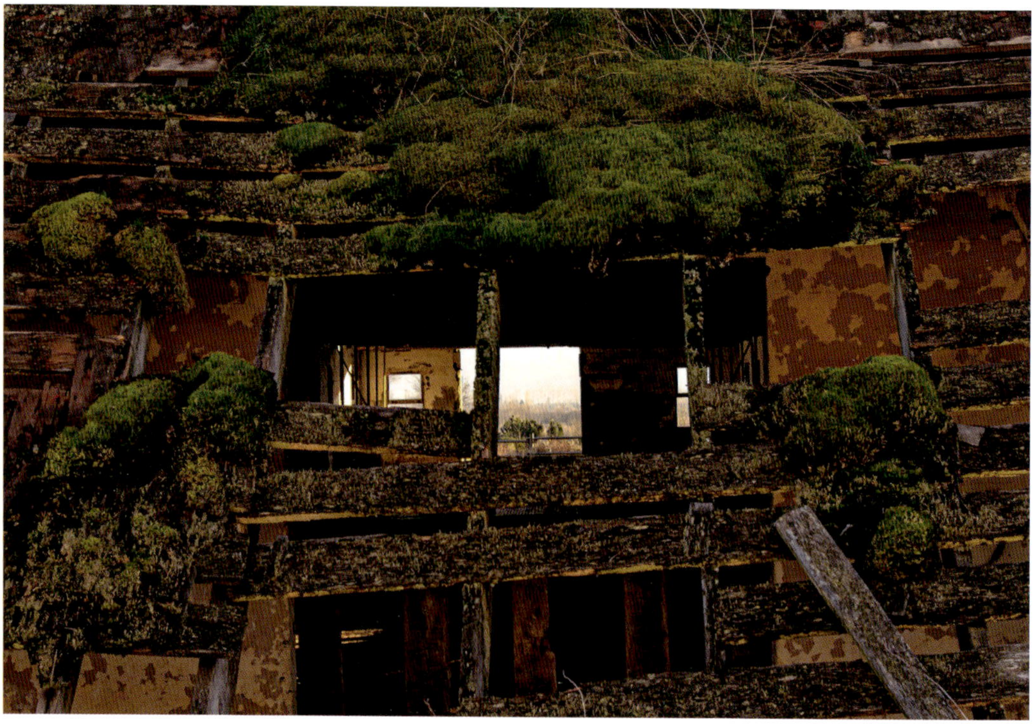

A narrow hallway with thorn vines, pebbles, and broken glass between barns.

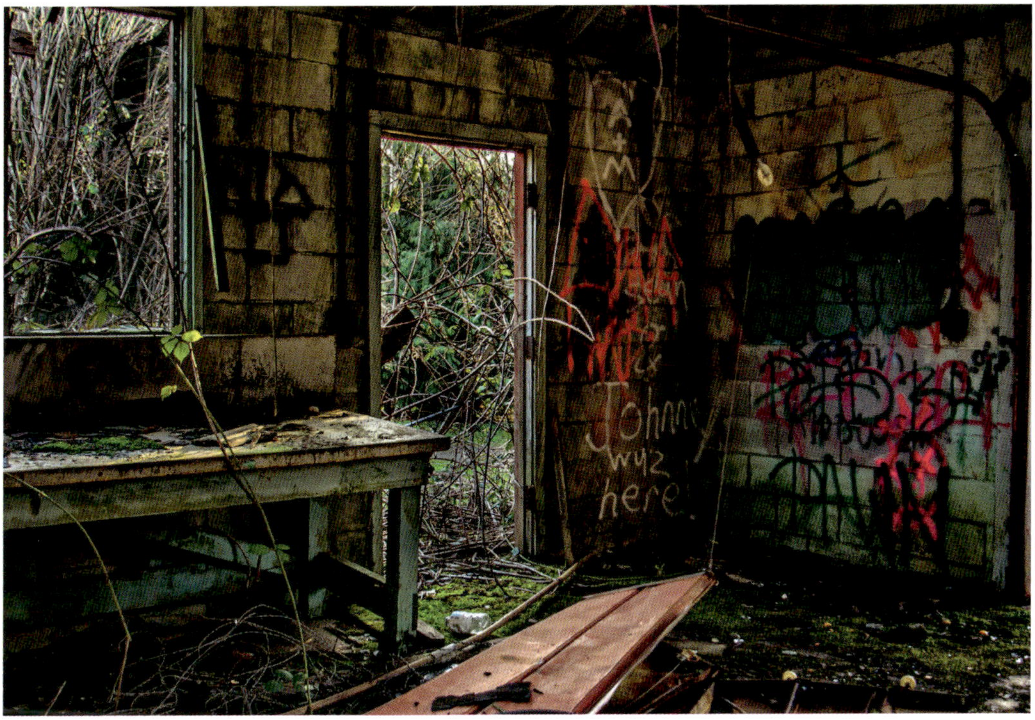

The North Cascades can be seen from all around the Northern Hospital campus, offering patients a beautiful escape from their work on the farm.

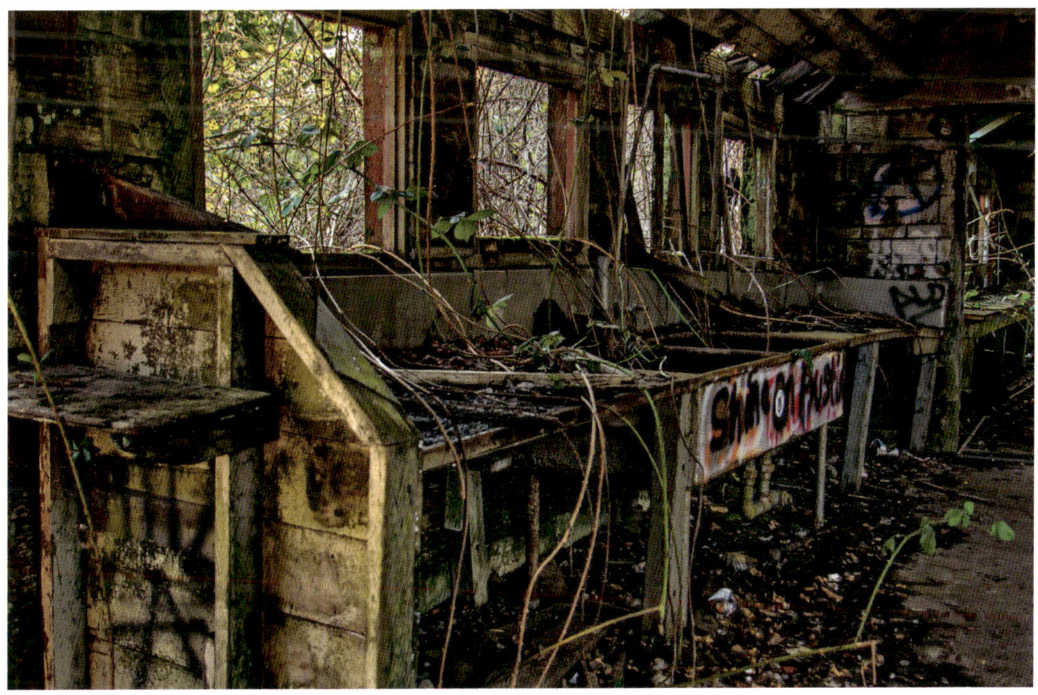

Layers of the property's infrastructure offer an idea on how the property was built in the early 1900s. Bricks and concrete of a multitude of colors show the wear and tear from the tests of the weather and age.

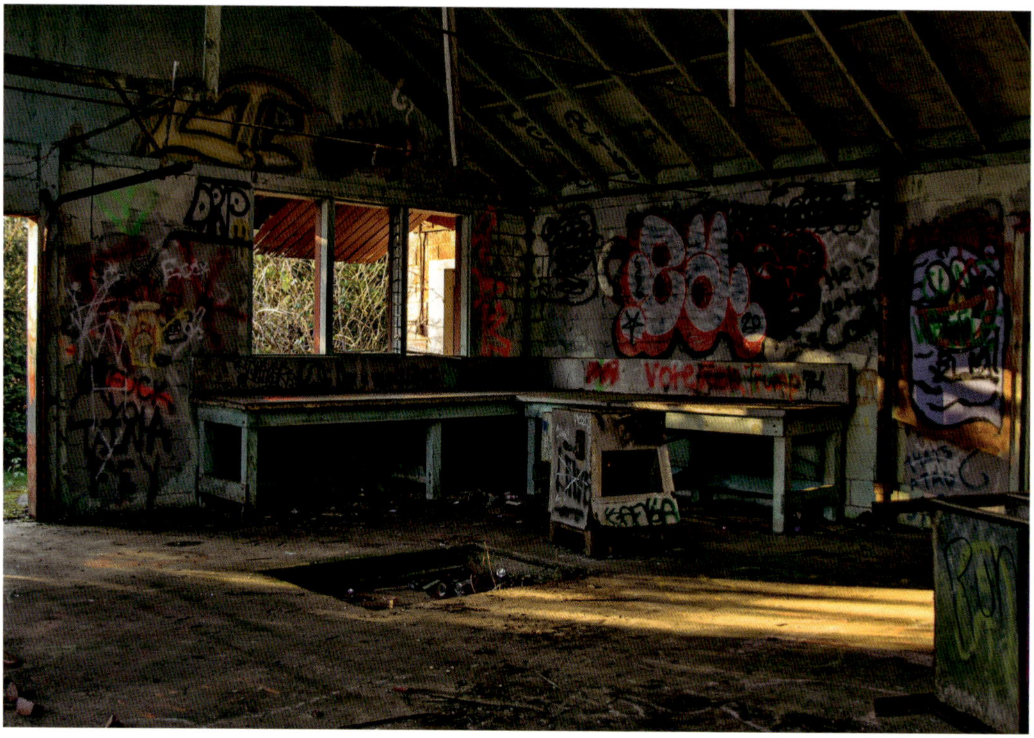

Some necessary dairy structures still remain, now a staple in time.

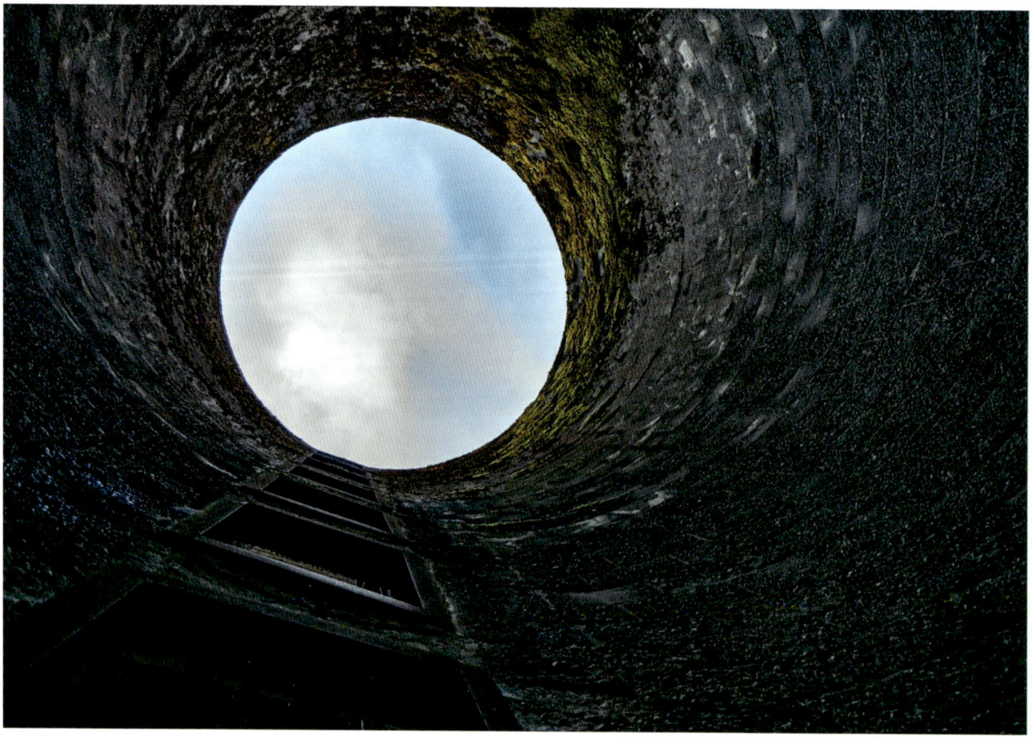

What is left of the silo on the farm has moss overtaking what was once there.

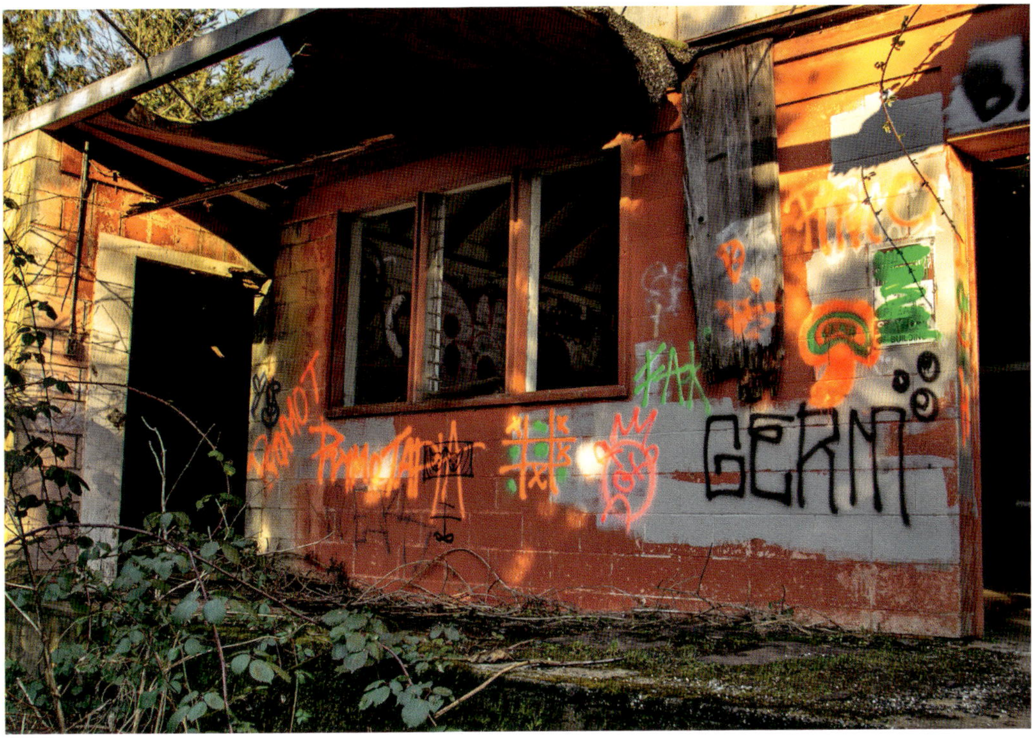

Golden hour hits upon the wood rotting beams in what looked like a structure that could have fallen any minute.

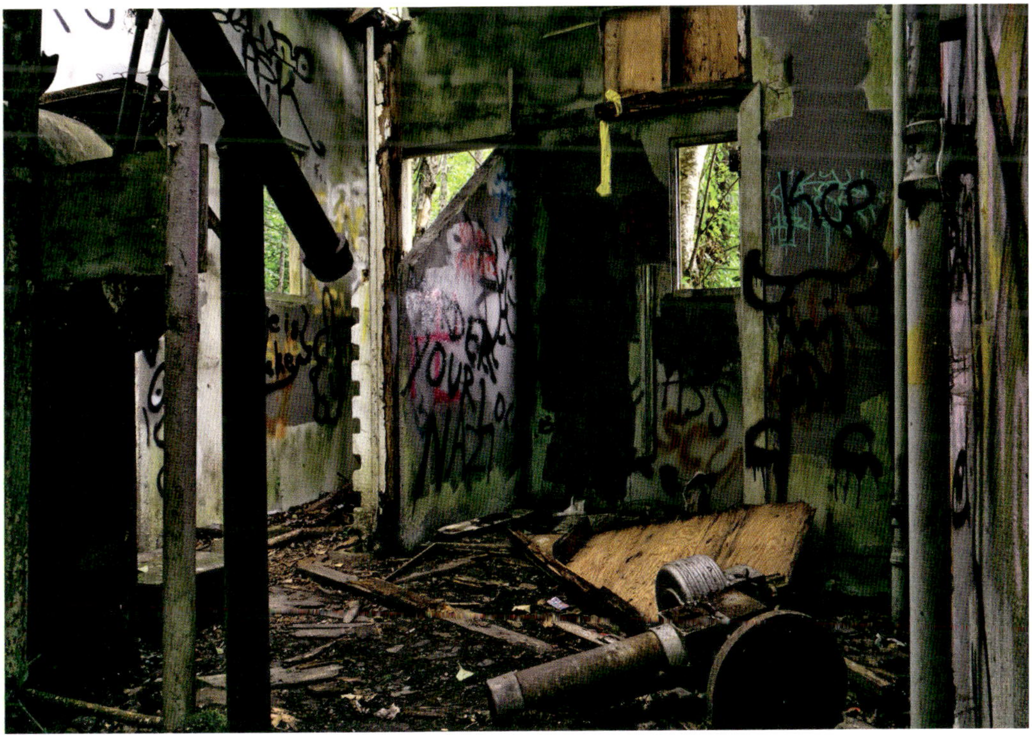

This structure appeared to be a cafeteria with steel serving tables overturned and windows to the kitchen area.

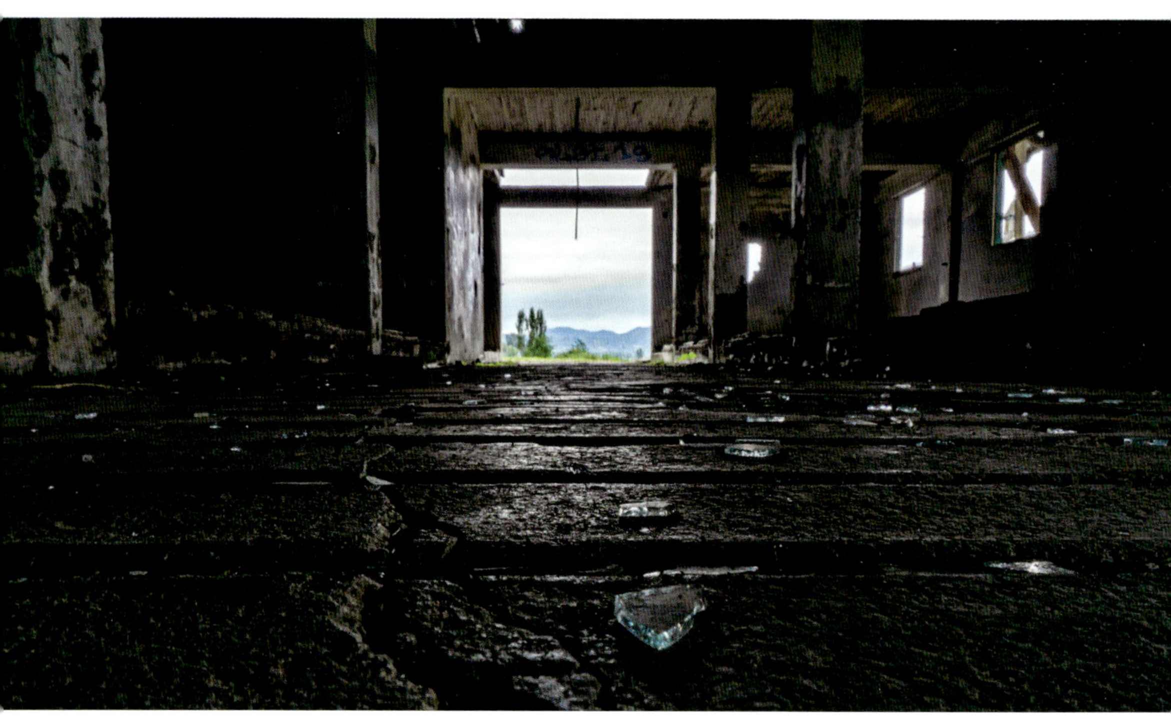

Broken glass among the horse barns where windows no longer remain and doorways provide wide entryways for the animals who once called this home.

When the hospital's doors closed, they found 240 containers of human remains left behind of cremated patients stored in the morgue. A morgue attendant had never gotten around to burying them. All the unclaimed ashes were buried in Hawthorne cemetery in Mount Vernon. On record, 1,487 patients died over the course of the hospital's lifespan. Unfortunately, most of the records pertaining to the burials were lost when the hospital closed, as record keeping was not to the extent as it is now today. There now are rumors of ghost stories about the property—most notable among the legends told is one of a little girl with a red ball and a male ghost searching for her.

The last century has played its course on how mental health has developed, becoming more of a political *status quo* topic of discussion. Quality of treatment and interest in promoting a healthier lifestyle for those who needed it became more adaptable. In the process, the United States began to deinstitutionalize as asylums became notorious for overcrowding, abuse of patients, lack of hygiene, and overall poor living conditions. The stigmas that came with mental health have slowly started to fade. Mental health has advanced its human rights, social movements, hygienic health, and treatments.

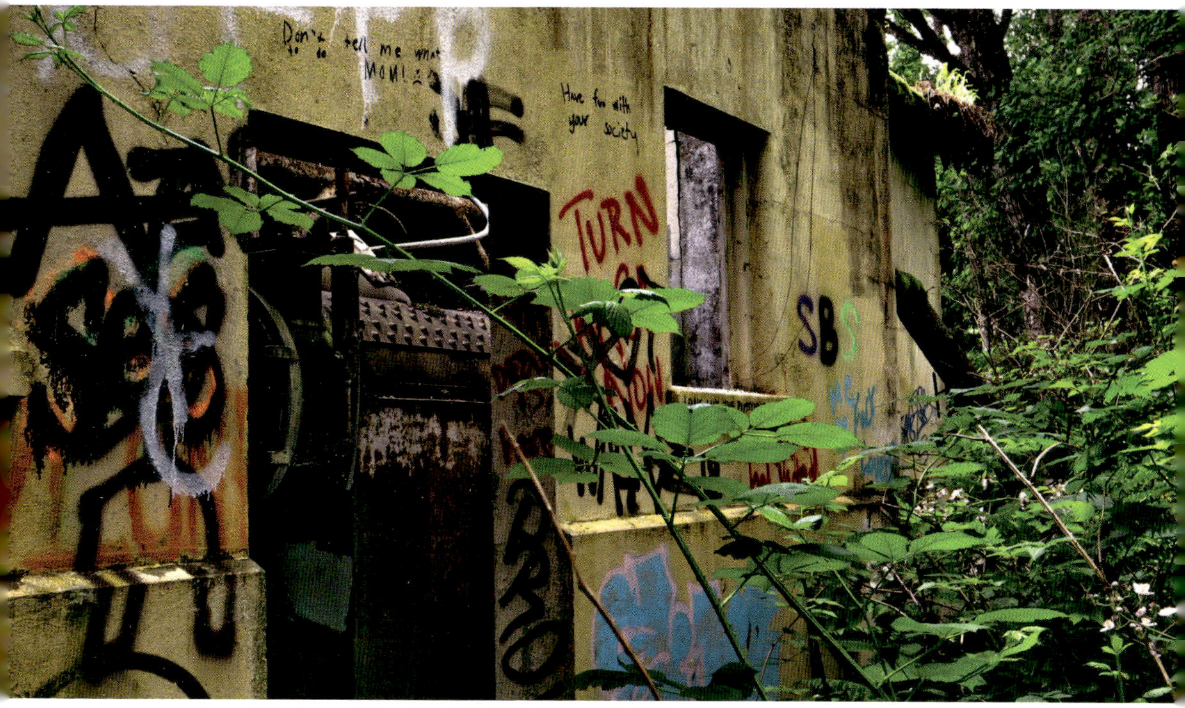

Blown-out windows remain on this deteriorated structure that sits in between the hospital and the farm.

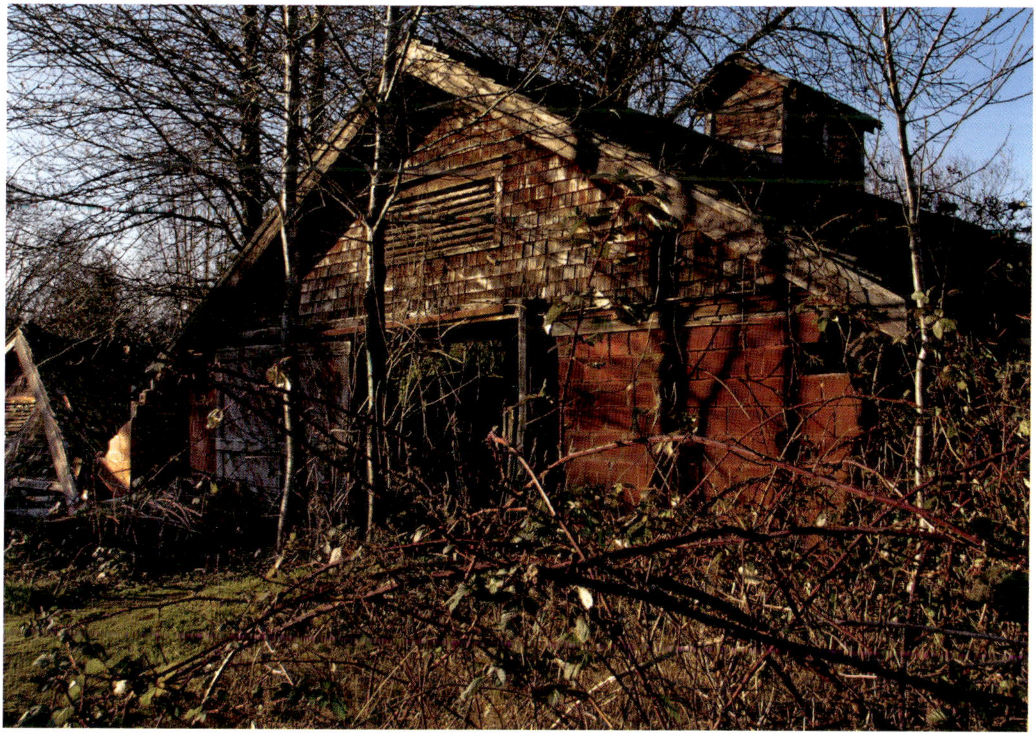

Plumbing was much different in the early 1900s, as this building's pipes are all towards the ceiling but disconnected in many areas—it has not faced the test of time well.

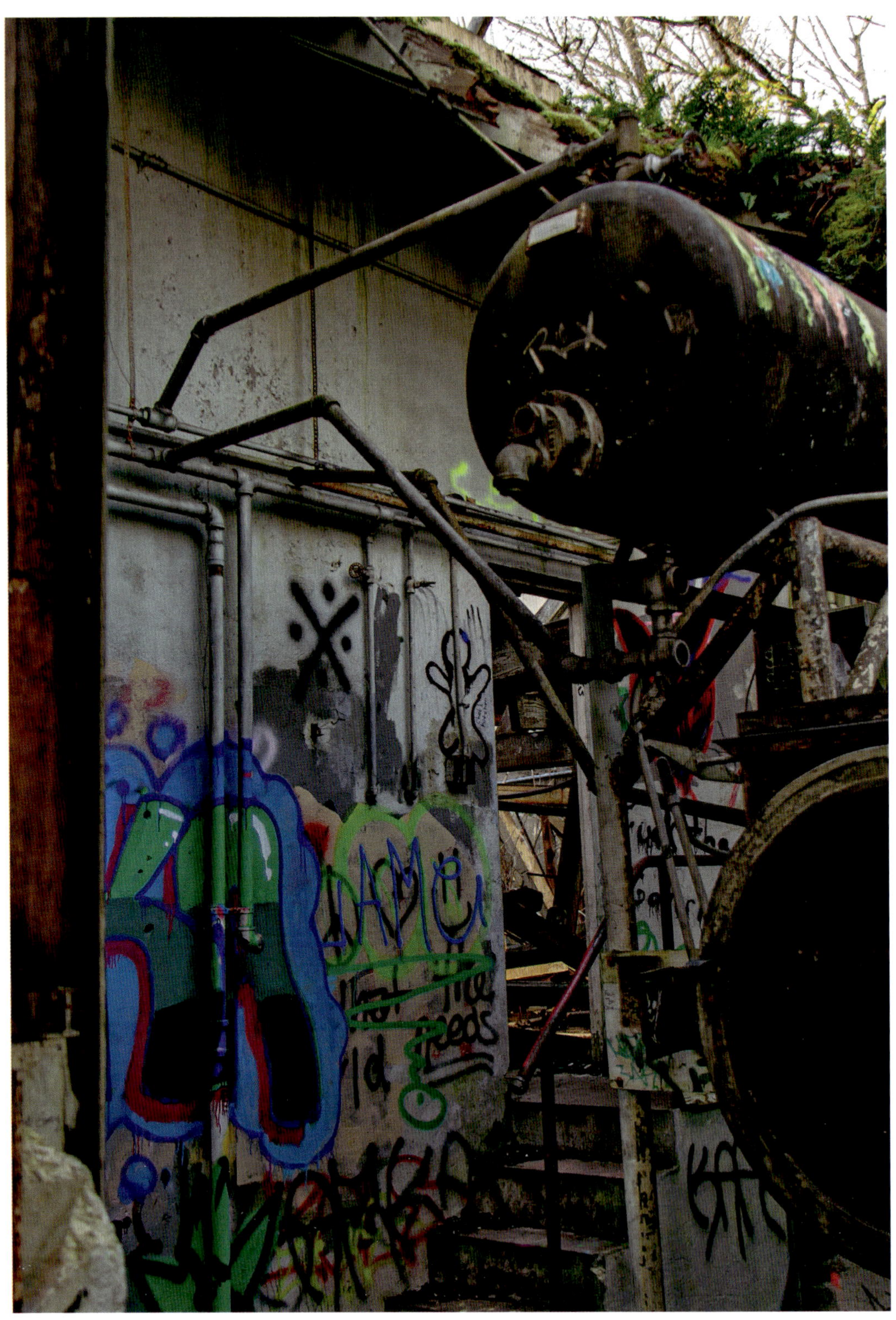

Northern Hospital's crematorium furnace operated from the 1920s to the early 1950s, now somehow still remaining intact.

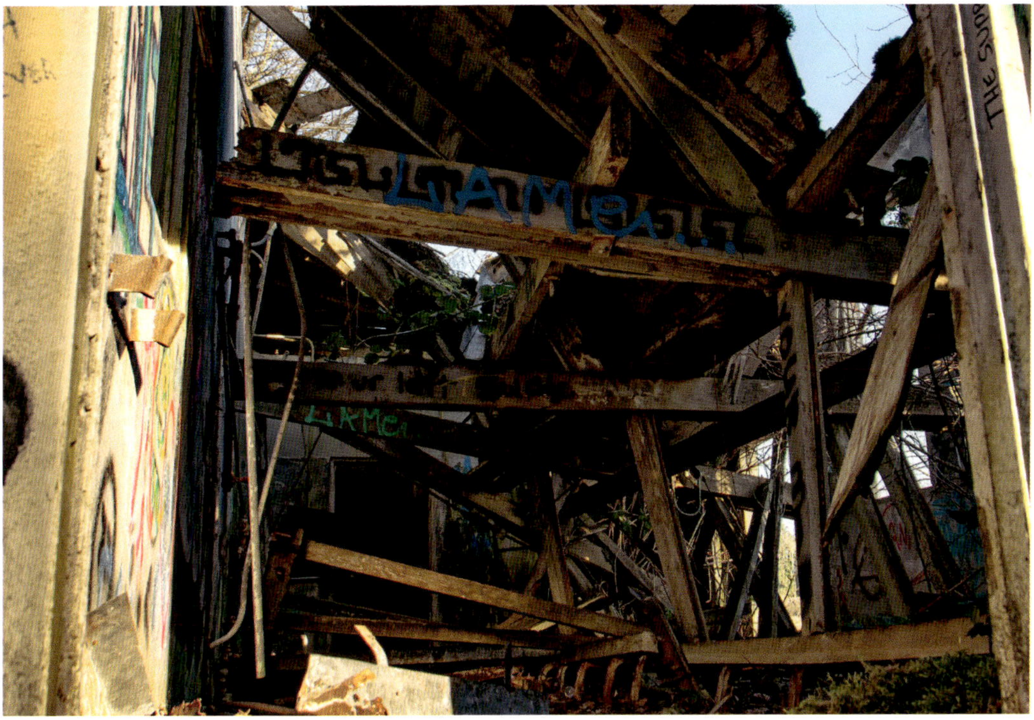

Ivy vines and fallen wooden beams take over what is left of the crematorium. Curious how many nail beams are actually keeping the structure still standing.

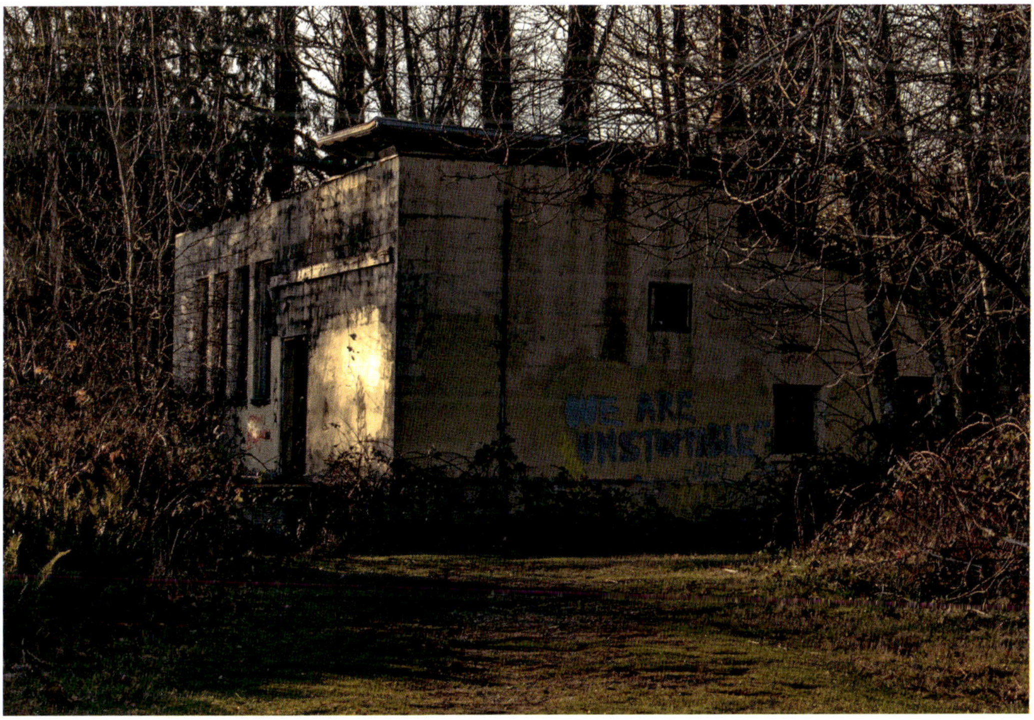

Up and close to the very eerie crematorium.

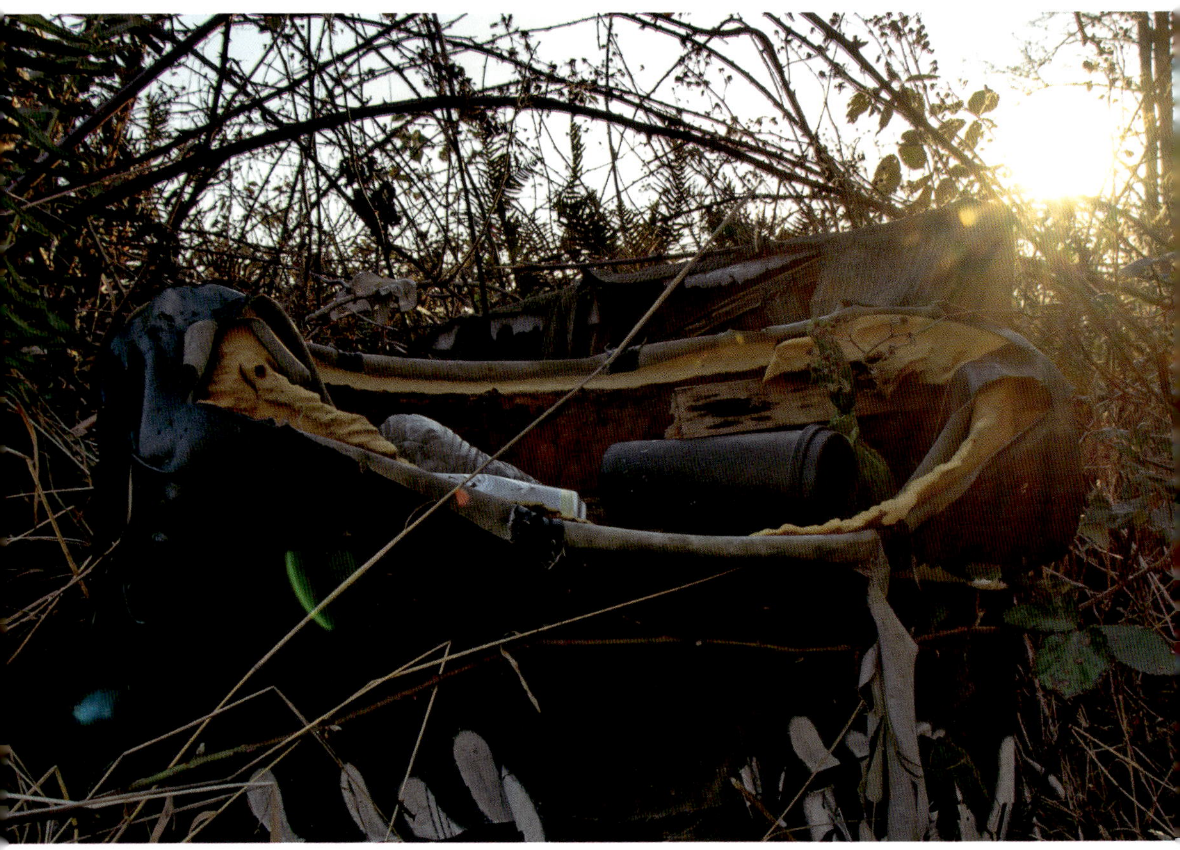

*Above:* After visiting this facility multiple times, one would have not known that this leather couch lived among the vines up until late 2020.

*Opposite page:* Some of the buildings on the campus have now dirt, debris, and leaves instead of flooring.

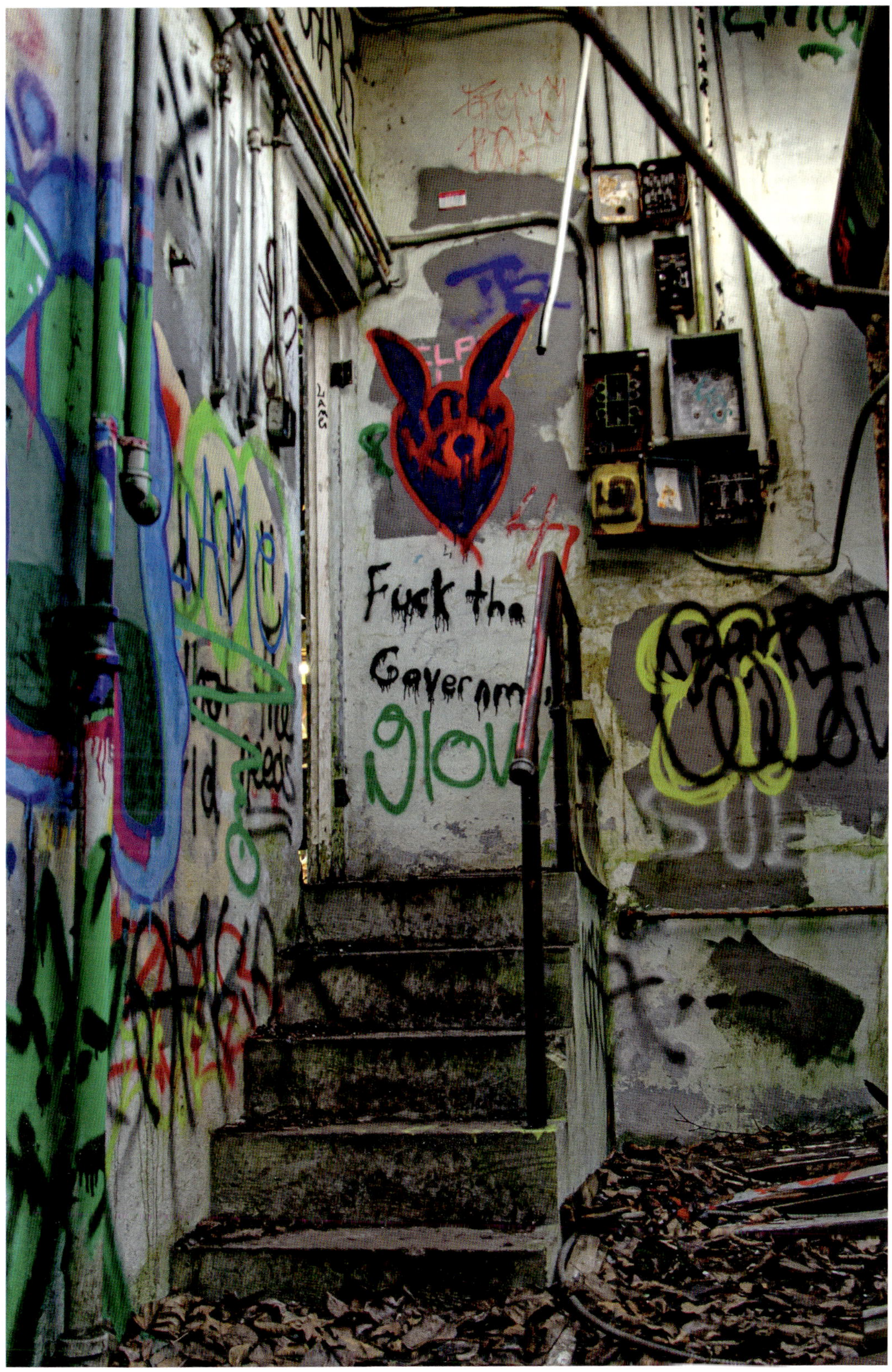
Fuck the

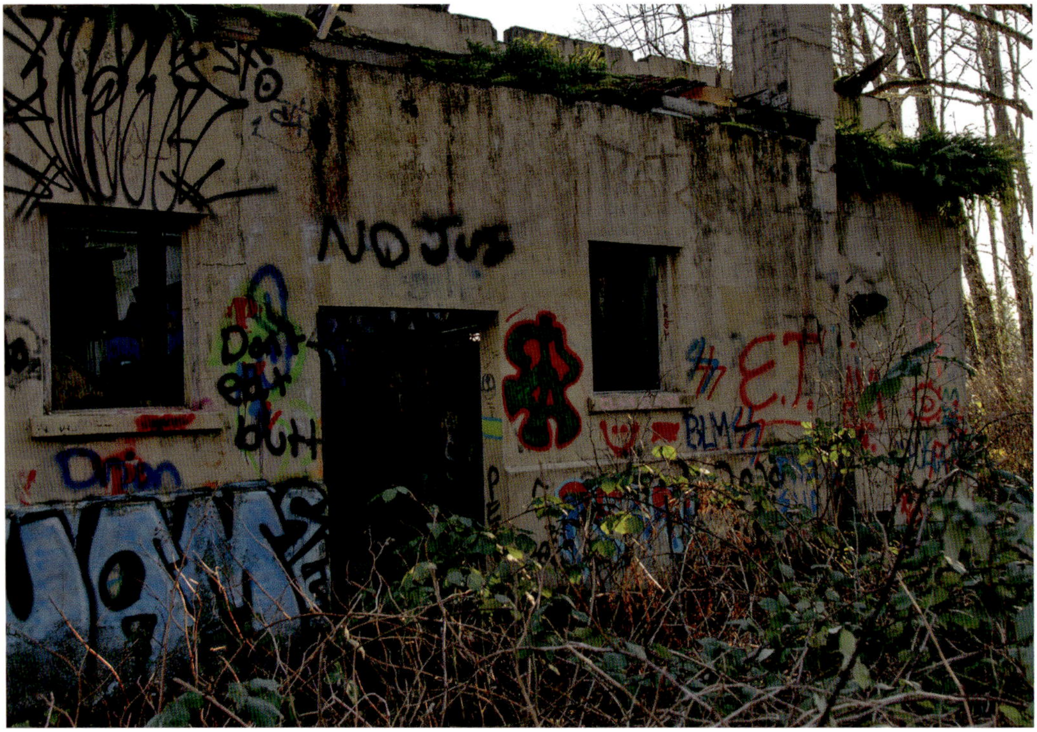

Northern Hospital's crematorium was closed when a local funeral home took over the funeral proceedings.

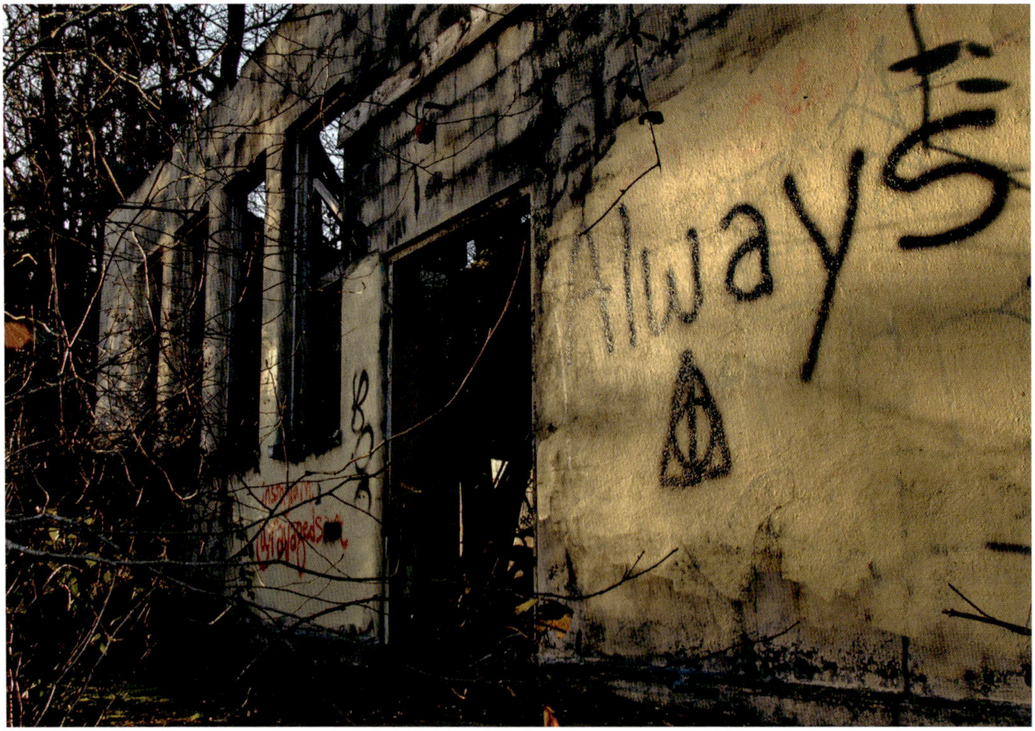

Spanish-style stucco design did not benefit the very wet climate for the property.

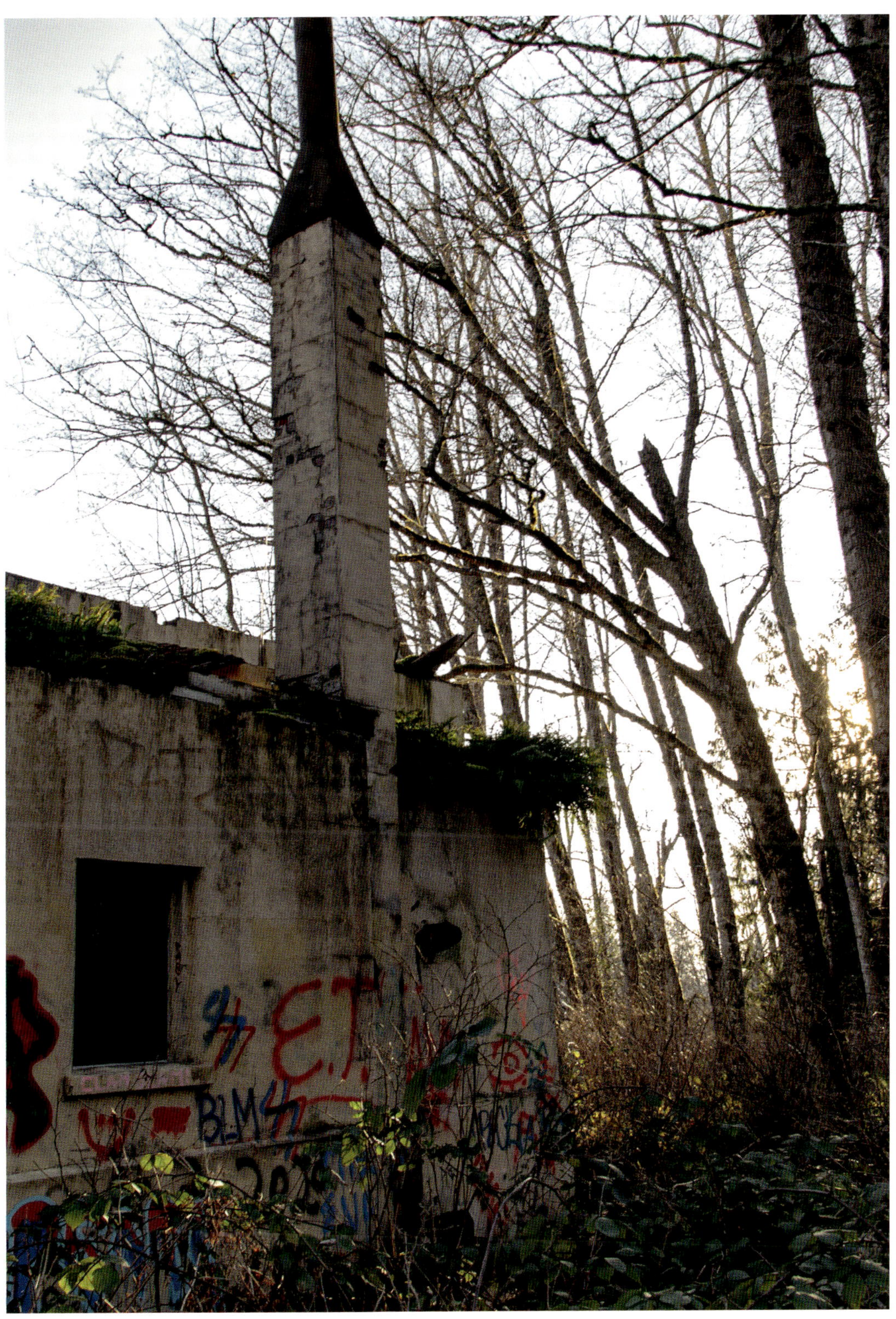


Hundreds of cremated remains were found in tin cans when the hospital closed; eventually, these ashes were laid in a mass grave at the Mount Vernon cemetery.

# FINALE

This northern route that runs almost parallel to the Canadian border has much more history than the buildings and cities built here 100 years ago. The region was first settled by Paleo-Indian Native Americans for more than 8,000 years. After the Gold Rush, settlers migrated north on the quest for what gold was left and trapped animals for fur. The actual pass that became the Cascade Pass was not built until 1895 to provide a clearer and direct route for travelers, fur traders, loggers, and miners. The road became beneficial to the locals industrializing their goods to make a good day's wage. After the road flooded the first time, three dams were constructed over the course of ten years, which caused an influx of tourism attraction to the area. Old highways were updated and/or combined to become the North Cascades Scenic Highway.

Laws changed in these areas, and within a decade, they closed overnight. The world no longer needed these businesses, but it holds truths and understanding of how past lives were lived. It is crazy to think that opening North Cascades National Park has now helped protect this land from ever being overdeveloped into a city landscape. Every federal land holds the secrets of the lands and sometimes you might get lucky and find an abandoned city of yesteryear.

Nature reclaimed these civilizations and they will continue to do it outside of our lifespan. Any building or location has the potential to become deserted—conventional wisdom says that over five years, any abandoned area can start to begin to look like a forest. Civilizations will collapse, buildings will hold a haunting beauty, and life will find a way.

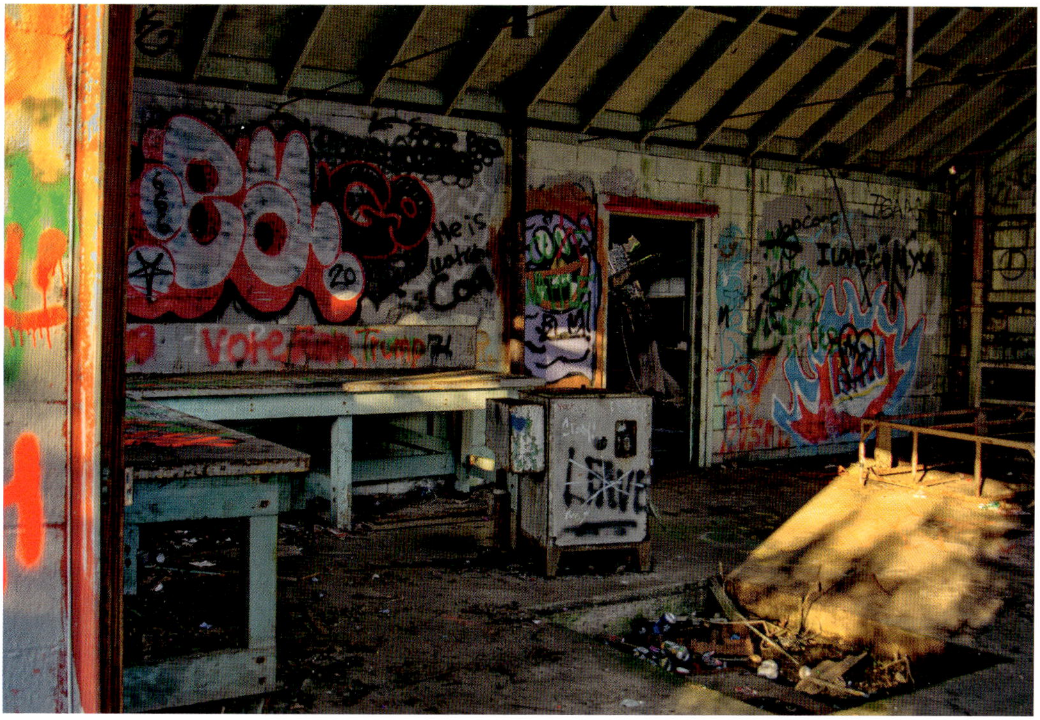

Partial roof remaining to staff quarters on the 700-acre farm.

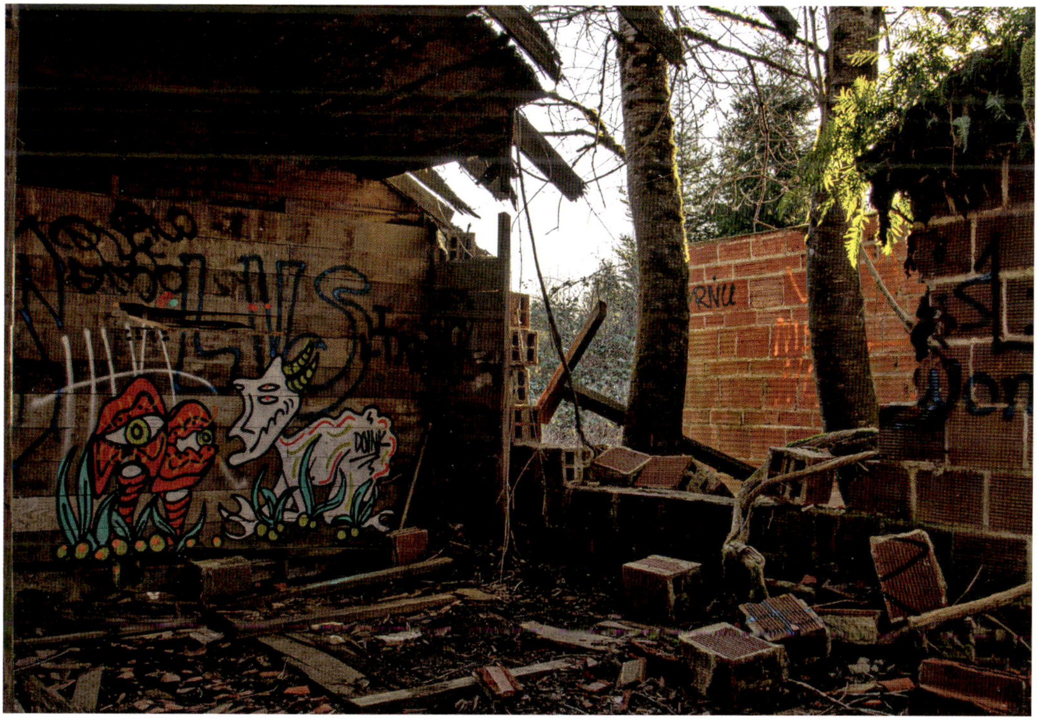

Some of these buildings surprisingly still had ceilings, roofs, and walls still. It is crazy to think one day everyone just up and left.

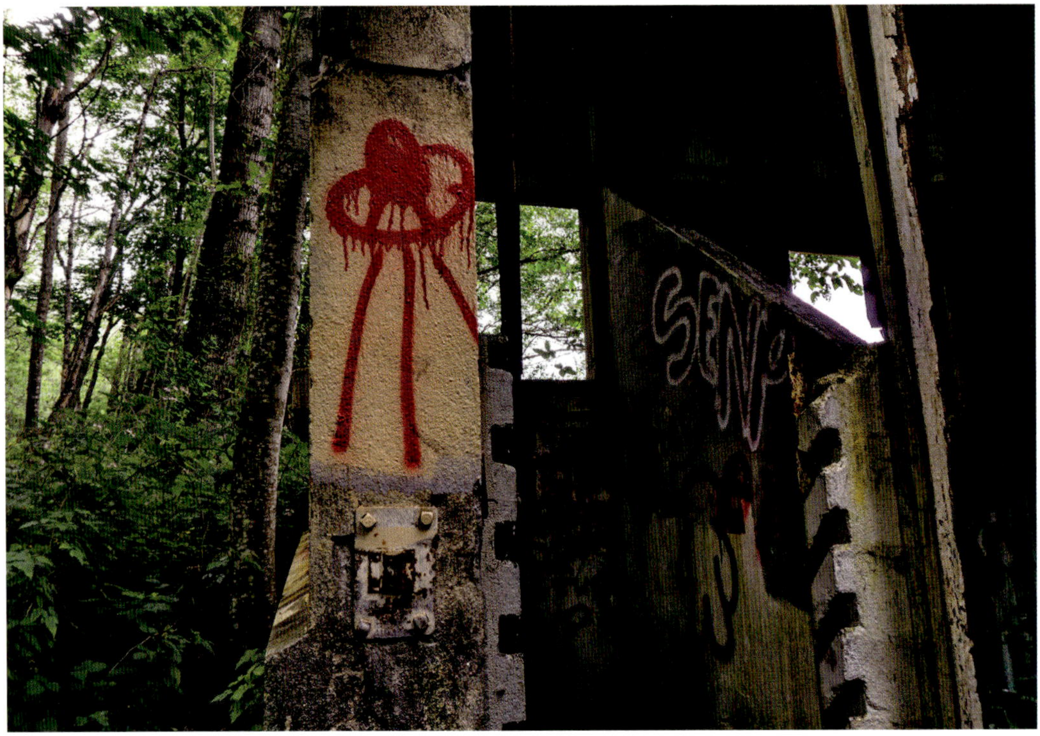

Old sinks overgrown with vines through windows, like nature was claiming it as theirs.

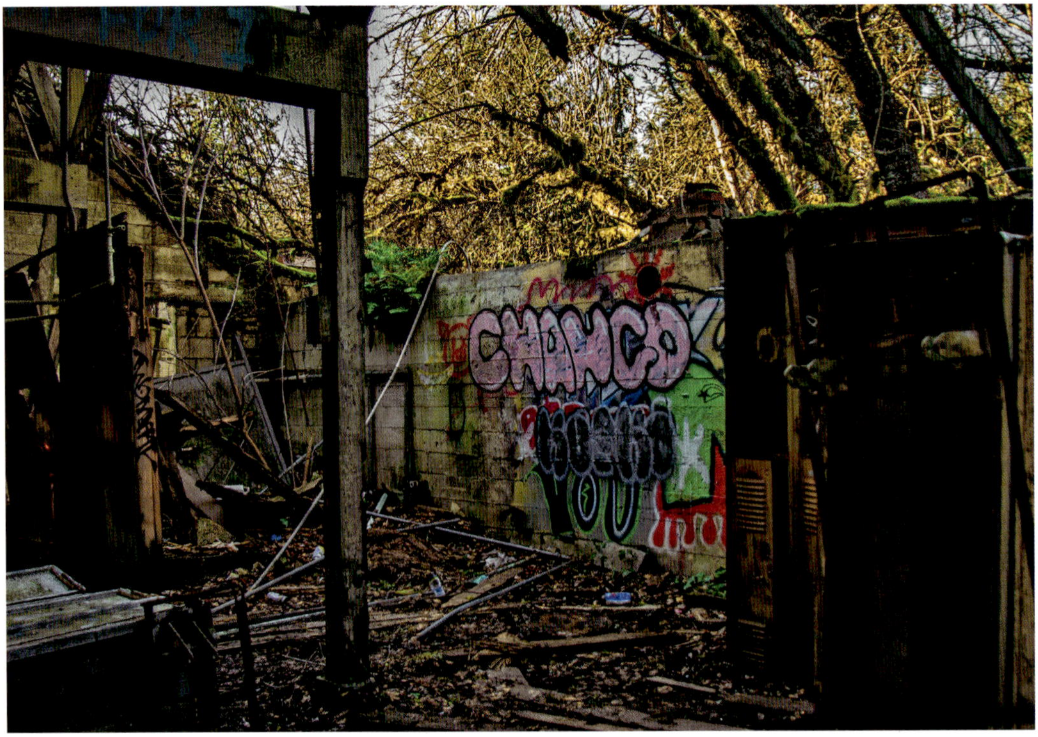

Dairy cows' entrance to dairy barn facilities. Their milk was provided to multiple hospitals in Washington.

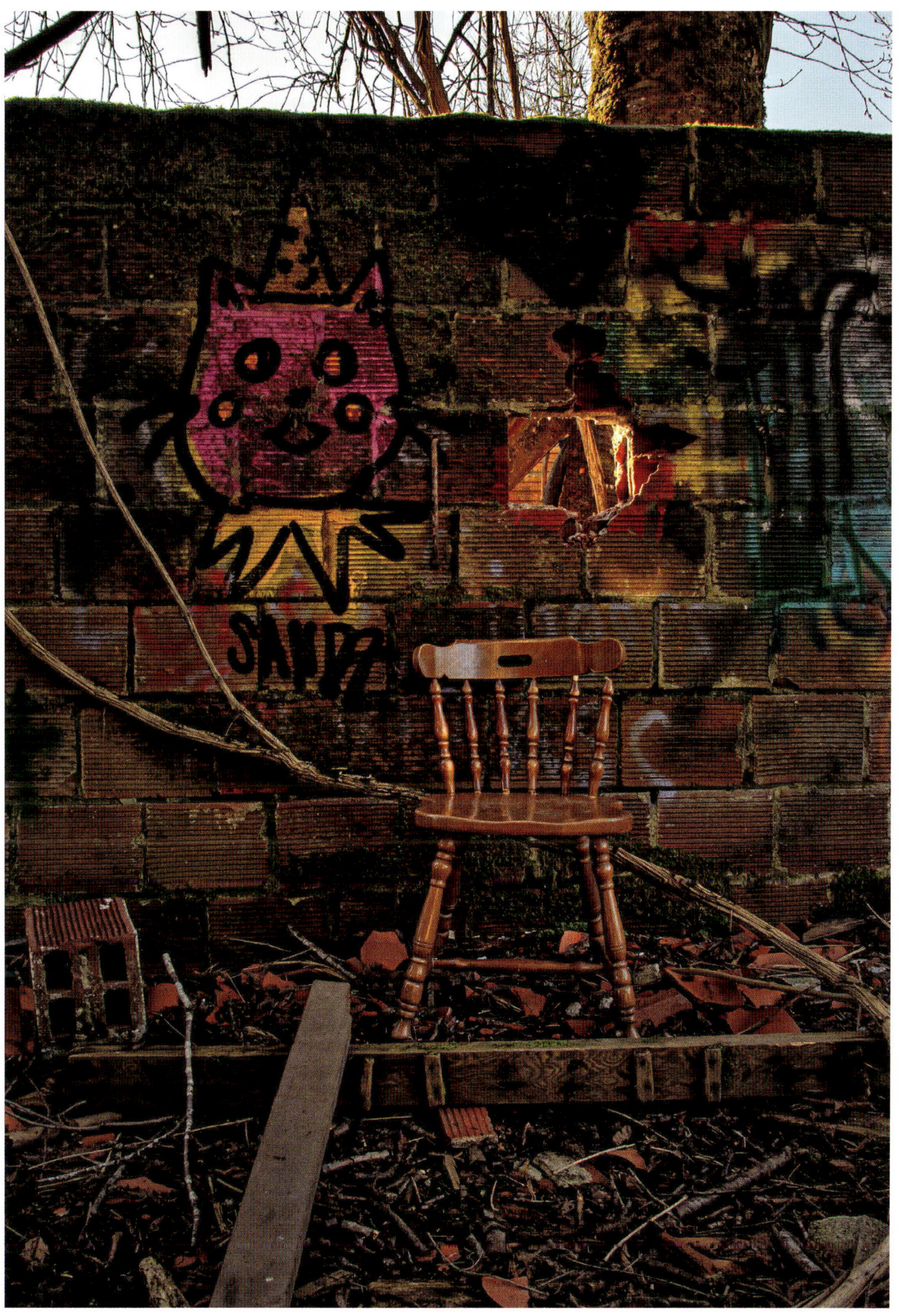

To urban explorers, finding anything that appeared to be intact always comes off as gold. Of all the things that remained in this area, this one chair lingered untouched.

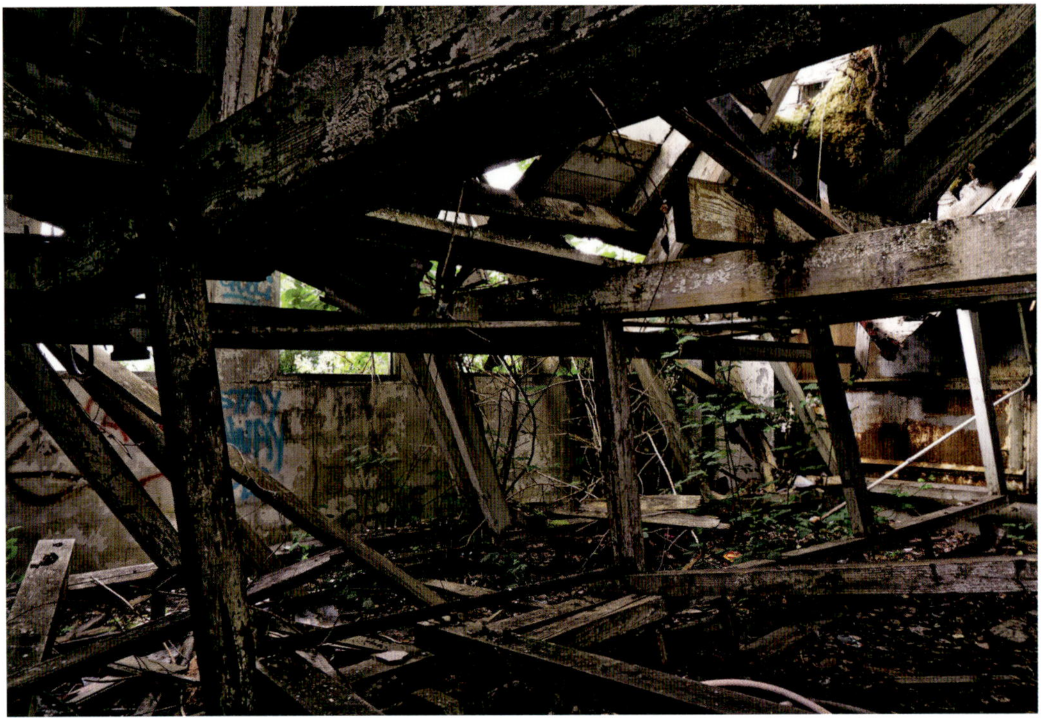

The cafeteria still had tables intact and attached to the wall, with vandalism art being overridden again and again as time decayed the structure even further.

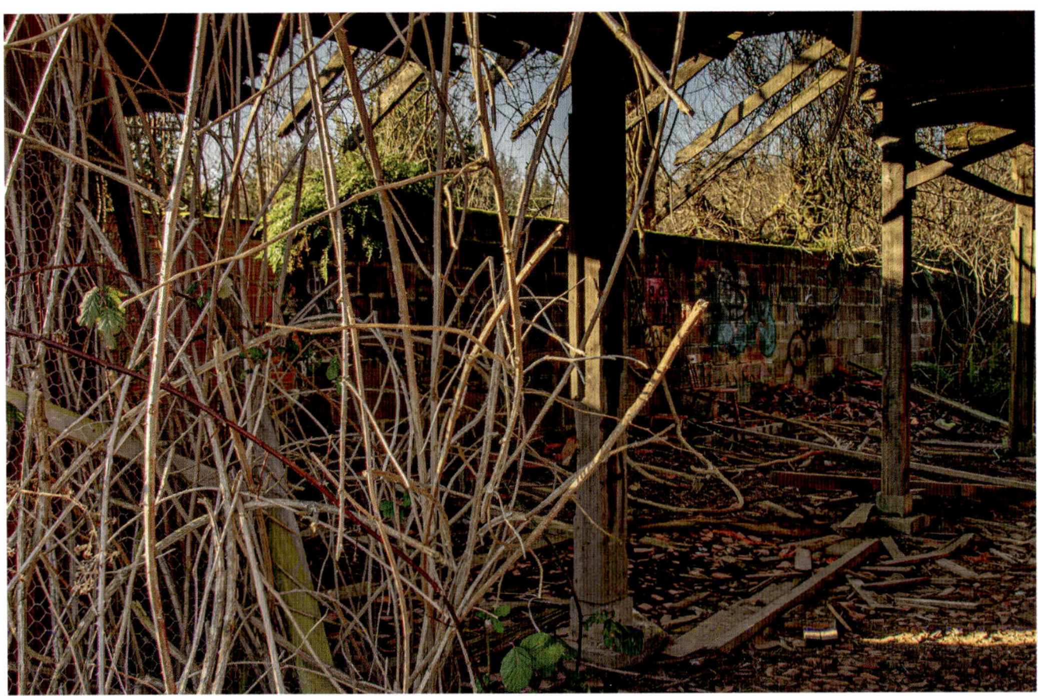

Some of these abandoned structures that remain on the facility are actually not noted in the history of the property and are quite a mystery.

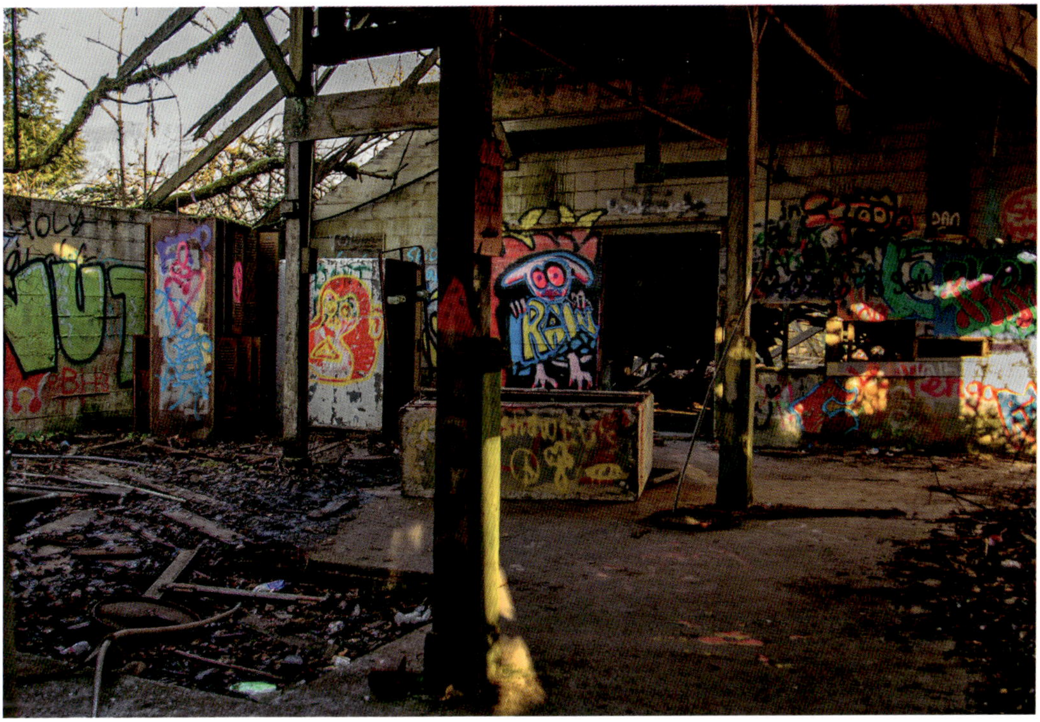

Staff housing had two buildings that still remained, or what was left of them. Trees ended up overgrowing throw walls and windows that once stood.

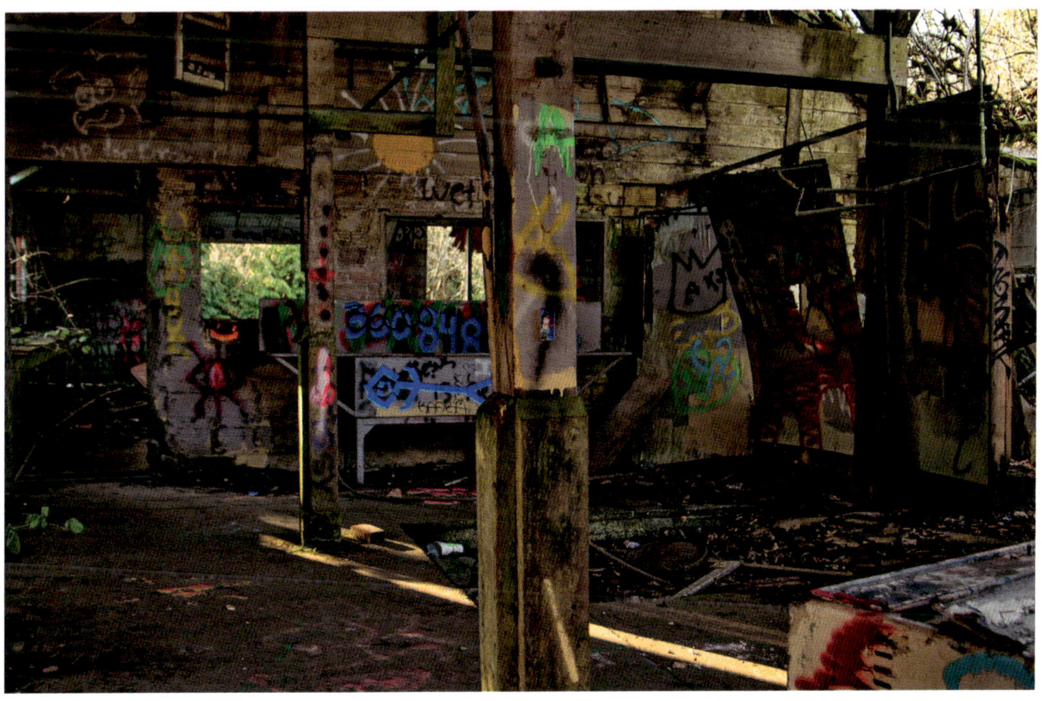

Staff working at the hospital had their own private facilities located in close proximity to the farms instead of the hospital.

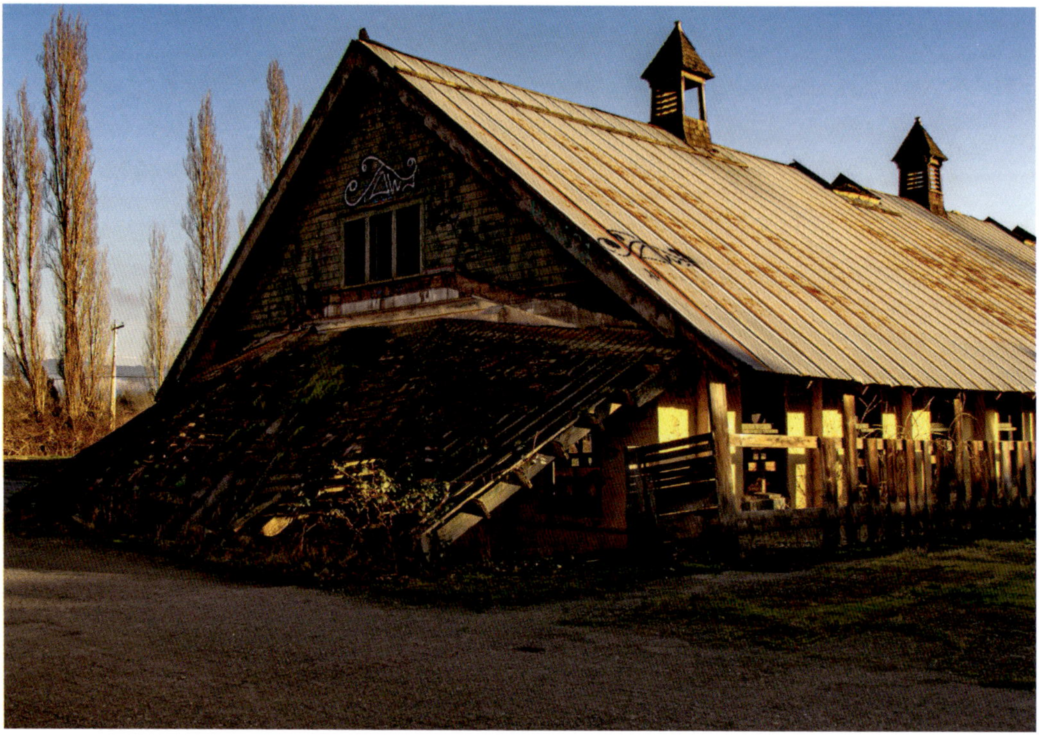

Barn, inclusive of the dairy barns, where patients would work; eventually, this south-end entrance collapsed in on itself.

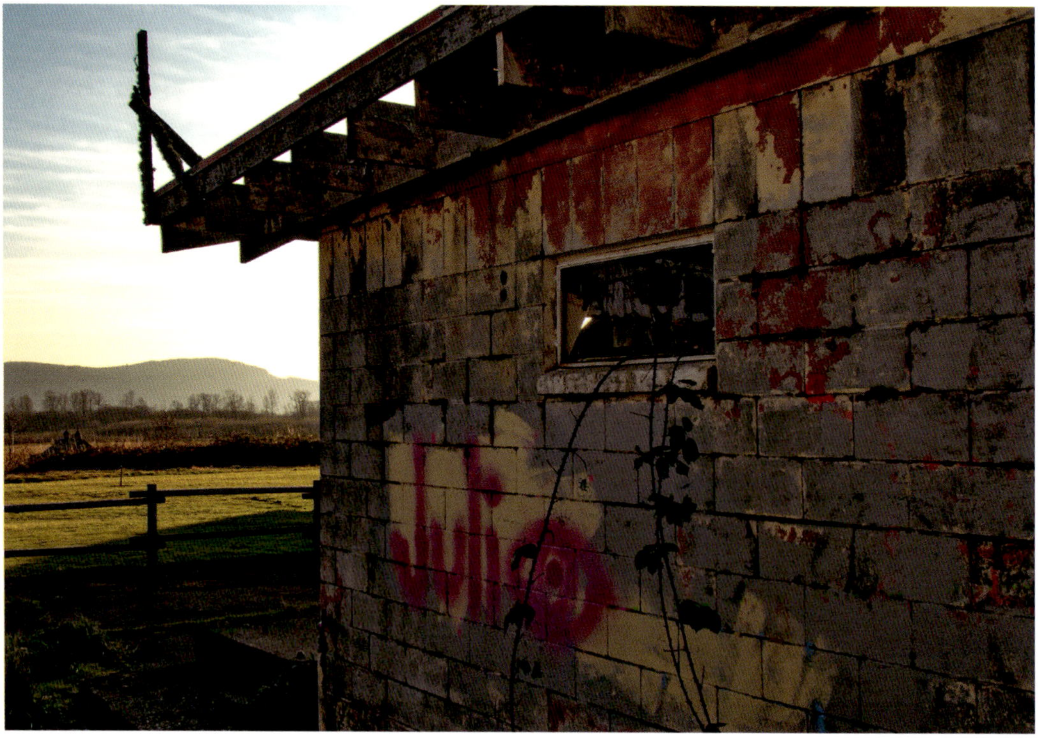

Entrance to the dairy barn where cows were kept to supply all the hospitals in the nearby areas.

Our social structures changed to make these buildings obsolete. In current times, we repair what is broken, and these buildings show the true get up and leave nature of migrating civilizations of our times. The social laws on mental health and how buildings were first constructed all end up intertwining on the main goal to preserve what nature is left of these areas. It seems that no matter how hard we humans try to create something, nature always finds a way to take it all back. And sometimes all that is left is to take a step back and admire this unstoppable force at work. Even though seeing nature slowly creep over manmade structures can make you question how temporary everything is surrounding us is, it is a beautiful sight nevertheless.

Throughout our lives, we will witness birth, we will watch buildings rise, we will experience unique once in a lifetime opportunities. However, on the contrary, we will face hardships, watch businesses close and buildings decay, and we will witness death. One is only able to understand or interpret the world based on the knowledge already observed and the experience already gained.

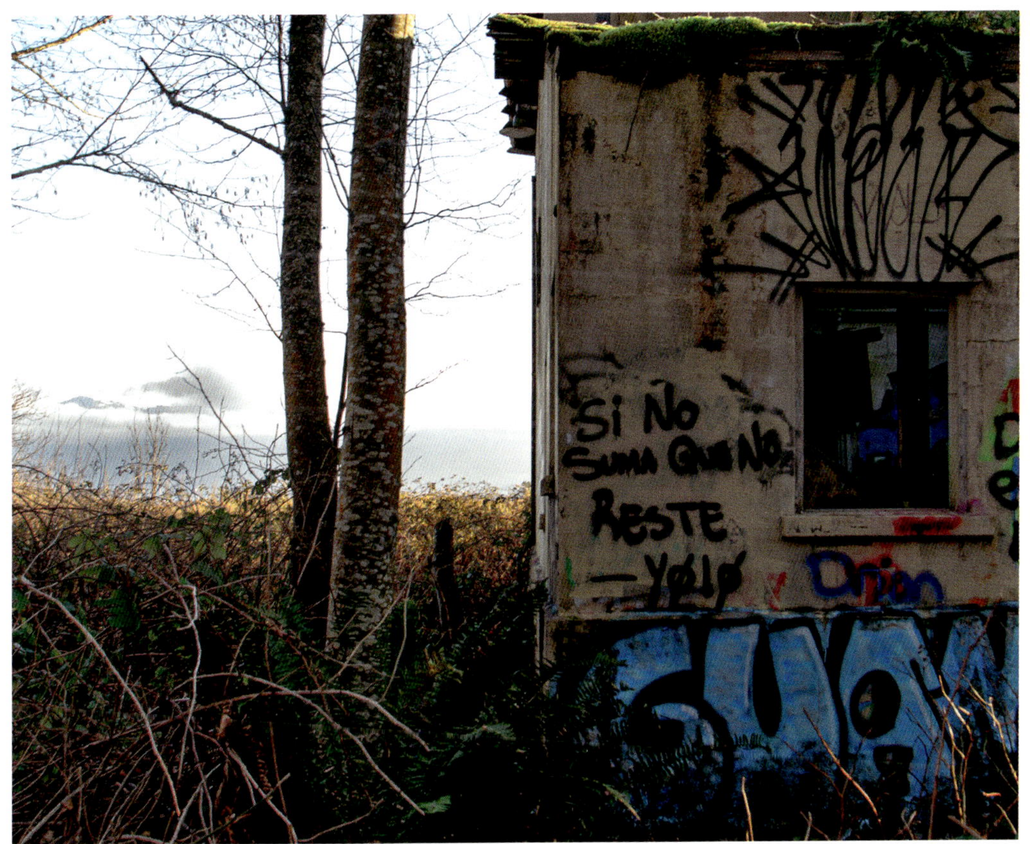


Mount Baker overlooking the Northern Hospital; its history will represent our ever-changing growth of knowledge for mental health for future generations.

# ABOUT THE AUTHOR

**Debra Huron** has been dedicated to the art of urban exploration photography before she even had a platform to post it on. Debra, also known as Deb, born and raised in Queens, NY, discovered her passion of taking print photography while pursuing her BA in corporate communications from CUNY Baruch over ten years ago. Since then, Deb's photographic eye has developed a style of her own with splashing a colorful display of decay. Deb shoots with a Nikon D610 and Sony Alpha a5000. She is a strong believer in collecting moments over possessions, as a picture is worth 1,000 words. Her desire to explore moments lost in time has taken her adventures and vacations to the most unexpected dilapidated and deteriorated places one would normally not call a "vacation." Aside from urbex photography, she used to shoot nightlife in New York City prior to relocating to the West Coast.

Deb currently resides in Portland, Oregon, with her boyfriend and dog, Marceline. Marceline is not a fan of exploring abandoned buildings, but they make it work. Follow her adventures on Instagram: @d3bsnaps.